Seeing the Face

of

God

*Memoirs of a Light-skinned
Black Woman*

Rosie Glapion

WESTBOW°
PRESS
A DIVISION OF THOMAS NELSON
& ZONDERVAN

Scripture quotations taken from the New American Standard Bible', Copyright © 1960, 1962, 1963, 1968, 1971, 1972, 1973, 1975, 1977, 1995 by The Lockman Foundation. Used by permission." (www.Lockman.org)

WestBow Press books may be ordered through booksellers or by contacting:

WestBow Press
A Division of Thomas Nelson & Zondervan
1663 Liberty Drive
Bloomington, IN 47403
www.westbowpress.com
1 (866) 928-1240

Because of the dynamic nature of the Internet, any web addresses or links contained in this book may have changed since publication and may no longer be valid. The views expressed in this work are solely those of the author and do not necessarily reflect the views of the publisher, and the publisher hereby disclaims any responsibility for them.

Any people depicted in stock imagery provided by Thinkstock are models, and such images are being used for illustrative purposes only. Certain stock imagery © Thinkstock.

ISBN: 978-1-4908-2374-4 (sc)
ISBN: 978-1-4908-2373-7 (e)

Library of Congress Control Number: 2014901410

Printed in the United States of America.

WestBow Press rev. date: 01/23/2014

Contents

DEDICATION

*This book is dedicated to Almighty God, Father,
Son and Holy Spirit to whom I give all honor,
glory, praise, adoration and thanksgiving.*

*It is also dedicated in loving memory
of Glenn Michael John Glapion, a most
remarkable man, the love of my life and my
darling husband of nearly 42 years.*

Preface

I give praise and glory to God for compelling me to write this book. In it I bare my soul to reveal how racial hatred is actually hatred of God and how this hatred has permeated every aspect of my life. Yes slavery was outlawed but the white supremacy that fueled the system continues to fuel racial hatred and discrimination. My experiences as a light-skinned African American woman in the 21st century United States of America can only be described as life on the new plantation. Racism is an evil system that white and African Americans must confront and overcome. Love conquers hate, more specifically, the love lived and preached by Jesus Christ: "I give you a new commandment: Love one another. As I have loved you, so you also should love one another. This is how all will know that you are my disciples, if you have love one for another." John 13:34-36. Prayer is a powerful weapon that we have to overcome hate.

We must, individually and collectively, never cease raising our hands to heaven beseeching God to change human hearts from hate to love. Only then will liberty, equality and justice flow over our nation from coast to coast. Not with man-made laws, not with armies, not with worldly might, only with God is this possible.

About the Author

Rosaria "Rosie" Glapion was born in Lake Charles, Louisiana. At an early age she entered a religious order of Catholic nuns. After leaving the religious order she earned a B.A. Degree from Xavier University in New Orleans. Later, she received a Master of Pastoral Studies Degree from Loyola University of New Orleans. She was married to Glenn Michael Glapion for nearly 42 years until he went to heaven on Monday December 3, 2012. She is a civil rights advocate and past president of the Lake Charles Branch NAACP (National Association for the Advancement of Colored People). She has received many awards for her social justice work in civil rights and for the community.

CHAPTER 1

For the Love of God

"Jesus said to him, you shall love the Lord your God with all your heart, with all your soul, and with all your mind. This is the greatest and the first commandment." Matthew 22:37-39

I was born October 10, 1946 in the deep-south city of Lake Charles, Louisiana. My mother told me that when I was born a rain shower passed by and that was supposed to mean a blessing. She also told me that when the nurse brought me to her the nurse asked "isn't she a cute little dibby? So for most of my childhood my relatives all called me Dibby.

I had a fairly normal childhood along with my three sisters and brother. We felt loved and safe. We were not rich but we never felt poor. We would ask our parents if we were poor but we never got a straight

1

answer. They both worked hard at their jobs to give us a good life. Daddy worked as a civilian employee for the government at an Army base in our area and mother was a nurse.

At a very young age I would enjoy laying out on the hammock in the back yard, writing poems. I would look up at the sky and the clouds and somehow I would feel the strong presence of God all around me. God enveloped me with the warmth and light of His presence. It was as though I had never left the warmth and the security of the womb. This strong closeness with God that I felt was distinct from religious training. I thought that this was a part of normal development for everyone – the bonding with God stage.

I went to public school until I was in the fourth grade and my mother could afford to send us to Catholic school. She wanted us to have a Catholic education.

There was only one Catholic school for colored children back then – Sacred Heart Catholic School. It was founded by Saint Katherine Drexel. She was born in Philadelphia, Pennsylvania and lived from November 26, 1858 – March 3, 1955. She was an American heiress, philanthropist, religious sister, educator and foundress. She dedicated her life and vast family fortune to the needs of oppressed Native Americans and African Americans. In 2000 she was canonized a saint by the Catholic Church. Sacred Heart Catholic School was run by the Sisters of the Blessed Sacrament an order of nuns founded by Saint Katherine Drexel. I will never forget those wonderful nuns. Not only did they impart knowledge to us but they taught us morals, courage and self-esteem. How ironic that white nuns strongly influenced the character and sense of self-worth of the colored and Indian children. We highly value the education and training we received from them for all of our lives and especially when the hell gates of hate would open upon us.

At first, as "colored" children we did not know that we were different from anyone else. It was only gradually that we came to the realization that there were white people and colored people and that the white people thought that they were better than us. We never understood why, we just knew they thought this. We did understand that this was based strictly on the color of our skin. We even wondered if there was a god for white people and a god for coloreds. Our mother would try to explain this to us, but we were really confused because our mother looked white. I myself looked white. But my other sisters and brother were different shades of brown. One of our sisters was darker than the rest of us and we asked our mother why our sister's skin was darker than ours? Well, she said, it is just like baking cookies. God left her in the oven a little bit longer. In our childish minds that was a good enough answer for us but we were actually jealous that God gave her more time than us. The same was true for our other relatives. My aunt would put my very, very blonde cousin in the stroller and go "to town" as we called it. Without fail, someone would stop to ask her whose child was she minding? She got so tired of it she decided not to take him to town with her anymore.

My mother made it very clear to us that no one was better than us and that we were all the same. She would say that we were not better than anyone else and that we were not less than anyone else. In those days the city buses had signs in them saying "coloreds to the rear". Our mother told us that she better not ever catch us sitting in the back of the bus because we are the same as anyone else and can sit wherever we pleased. She threatened to whip our butts if she ever caught us riding in the back of the bus. So we just avoided riding the bus altogether. We actually feared what our mother would do to us more than what the white folks would do.

Going to Catholic school in the fourth grade built upon the closeness I felt with God before learning the Catechism. The more I learned, the more I wanted to learn. I felt very much rooted in this world of space and yet I was very drawn to reach beyond this world. Many years later I learned that the dynamic of our existence of spirit in world, in a unity that cannot be divided, demands that we function at a level beyond our human existence. We know that our destiny is beyond the purely human and we strive for actualization beyond our creatureliness.

As a child I was not trying to solve the mysteries of the universe but I needed answers to some basic eternal questions like - who is God and who am I? Who is Jesus Christ? What is grace? What is sin? What is salvation? Am I saved? I found a lot of my answers in the old <u>Baltimore Catechism</u>. Basically it stated that the Alpha and the Omega decided to share His greatness and created a great world and a great universe. St Paul says in Romans 1:20 "Ever since the creation of the world His invisible nature, namely His eternal power and deity, has been clearly perceived in the things that have been made." Looking around His world which reflected His greatness, His love compelled Him to share this with a creation that could appreciate and share in all of this greatness. Therefore, he created man and woman in His own image and likeness, endowing them with His very own spirit (a soul) and free will. When a test of free will came along, humankind failed miserably (original sin). The creature turned away from the creator (sin). The creator, with a broken heart, longed to have the creature back in His bosom. The creature continued to resist. The creator even sent His human self (Jesus Christ) to show the wayward creature the way back to the creator's bosom. The creature continues to resist. In very simplistic terms this was my age-old Catholic belief.

The rites of passages of the Roman Catholic Church: Baptism, Penance, First Communion, Confirmation, and Marriage structured and impacted our lives and our experiences, individually and as a family. The Catechism states that Sacraments are "powers that come forth" from the Body of Christ, which is ever-living and life-giving. They are actions of the Holy Spirit at work in His Body the Church. We did not verbalize all of this but when a baby was born in our family we knew that the baby had to be baptized in the Catholic Church. Mostly, we knew that we were all Catholics and that we got that way through Baptism. For any new members to join us in being Catholic they had to be baptized. Infants had to be baptized as soon as possible. I clearly recall my grandmother becoming very upset with any parents in our family who delayed having their baby baptized. We knew that Baptism was a holy ritual that took away original sin. The ritual gave us a sense of belonging and acceptance by the church.

Penance, Confession, or the Sacrament of Reconciliation, as it is called today, also played an important part in our lives. We received first Penance in preparation for our First Holy Communion. I remember the nuns thoroughly drilling us in the liturgical ritual. My conception of sin was almost exclusively limited to telling lies. I knew if I told a lie I would have to go to Confession, tell God that I was sorry, ask forgiveness and promise God that I would not tell lies anymore.

For First Holy Communion we always had big family celebrations. Even our distant relatives came for First Communion celebrations. It was a big occasion for taking pictures for our family albums. All of the little girls in white dresses and veils gave the occasion a heavenly aura.

I had already experienced God's presence in my life and the sacraments of the church intensified the experiences. We can explain away the rituals. We can theologize about the meaning and purpose of the sacraments but I am hard pressed to find words to describe the actual experience. All of the book knowledge in the world cannot help a person understand the meaning of the sacraments in their lives until they have experienced being a new creation in baptism, reconciled with God, one self and others in Penance, and the incredible reality of Jesus taking possession of our being in Holy Communion. It is like reaching out and touching a little bit of heaven. For me, words are inadequate to describe these most profound moments of the soul bonding with the very source of its existence.

I have come to see that it is more characteristic of African Americans than most other people, including

Native American Indians, to experience God outside of formal, structured religion. Even though we were practicing Catholics we sang all of the old Negro spirituals or what some now call black Gospel. Our history of slavery etched these songs on our souls. The songs tell the story of relationships with God that were so deep they could withstand the forces of hell: "Do Lord Remember Me," "Wade in the Water," "The Gospel Train," and many more. We knew that there was no way to survive oppression, discrimination, racism without the mighty, mighty God sustaining us every minute of everyday of our lives. With these conditions, God could not be an occasional encounter for us. God had to be the very breath of our existence or we could not endure it.

My parents were vocal in standing up against the evils of racism and discrimination in our little community. They were very active in the NAACP (National Association for the Advancement of Colored People). My daddy was President of the local branch and my mother was Secretary. The Ku Klux Klan burnt a cross in front of our house. My parents always put us children to sleep in the bedrooms in the back of the house and they slept in the front in case our house would be fire bombed. Once some men brought a young black child to our home (he was not more than 10 years old). They wanted to show my parents where the police had repeatedly banged the child's head against a brick wall. Black soldiers came to our home to say that they went to a nearby bar for a drink and were told that they do not serve (n word). My daddy went to that bar, sat down and ordered a drink and they told him the same thing that they do not serve (n word). My daddy replied "that's ok because I do not drink (n word)." They all had a laugh and they served him and the soldiers ever since. Once we went to Mass at a Catholic church in a neighboring parish and were told that we would have to sit in the "colored" section. Even though we encountered racism and discrimination in our own church we could not let it move our faith in a powerful God who is greater than human weakness. Our faith transcended the evil actions of human beings. St. Paul asks in Romans 8:35: "What will separate us from the love of Christ? Will anguish, or distress, or persecution, or famine, or nakedness, or peril or the sword?" In spite of racism we remained devout Catholics who loved the church and the sacraments. Our faith was tried by fire and we were nailed to the cross with Christ. We strongly identified with the cross of Christ. Like Jesus on the cross we were stripped of all human consolation, leaving us naked with only God to cover us. Our nakedness was mirrored in the cross, rather His nakedness was mirrored in us. From songs like "Steal away, steal away, steal away to Jesus. Steal away, steal away home. I ain't got long to stay here" we developed a strong sense of happiness with God in the hereafter since we were already living in extreme torment. This is the soul of black folks that I try to explain to people who do not have the same history and experiences. God was the only hope of survival for our African ancestors in those cotton fields, tobacco fields – enduring a fate worse than death. That they survived is monumental testament to their faith. All African Americans of faith understand that in spite of pain, our inner peace, love hope, family, and friendships are strengthened by a force greater than any power on this earth.

The nuns who taught us in school always spoke of the love of God. Even with the closeness that I felt with God I needed to know more and I felt like I was missing something. I was determined to find out all I could about the love of God. I was very close to the nuns at school, especially because one of the nuns and I had the same name – Rosaria. She took me under her wings and was determined that I should be a nun. They encouraged me to join a religious order and to become a nun. At the age of 15 years old I applied to join an order of nuns up the country. They turned me down because they did not accept "colored" applicants. One day, in the school library, I found a book that showed an order of nuns who worked with the Catholic press and since I was very interested in journalism I thought this would be perfect for me. I applied and they accepted me. Two nuns came to the house to take me by train all the way to Boston, Massachusetts. I was very happy on the train and thought to myself "I am finally going to understand what those nuns mean by "the love of God."

CHAPTER 2

Out of the Wilderness

"As the deer longs for streams of water, so my soul longs for you, O God. My being thirsts for God, the living God. When can I go and see the face of God?"
Psalms 42:2-4

It was the first time I was out of the deep-south. I adjusted quickly to convent life. I loved the spirituality. I loved the austerity but when my first Christmas away from home came I was very homesick. I told the nuns that I had to go home for Christmas and that I would be back right after Christmas. They said "We do not go home for Christmas." All of the novices in my age group, from around the country, wanted to go home for Christmas. We were all homesick. Then came the first snowfall and, I from the deep-south, had never seen so much beautiful snow on the trees and the hillsides. Besides the nuns told us that Baby Jesus would bring us some nice things for Christmas and so we got over it. I graduated from high school in the convent. At the same time I learned how to print books and magazines on a big four-color offset printer. I even wrote a book for a children's series which the nuns published. For over six years I professed temporary vows of poverty, chastity and obedience. I was the perfect nun and I fully expected to stay there until the day I died. Even though I was the only "colored" nun in that order, I never experienced any difference between me and the other nuns. I think this is because I am light-skinned and there were nuns from Sicily who were very dark skinned. I mostly printed books and went to college classes while some nuns never went to college and were sent out to sell books door-to-door. At some point it was decided that I should get out more and one Saturday I was sent out with another sister to sell books door-to-door. Around noon time we stopped at a lady's house to eat our sandwiches and use the bathroom. The bathroom was upstairs and when I came back down stairs the lady said to me "put back whatever you took." Of course this was a shock to me. She evidently thought I had stolen something. Of course I did not but when we got back to the convent and reported it I was never again scheduled to go sell books door-to-door again.

These were times of major racial unrest in the 1960's. We never watched television and once in a while they would put the news on the radio during dinner. On this particular night the news was reporting how the colored people were burning down their neighborhood in Roxbury, Massachusetts in response to the assassination of Dr. Martin Luther King, Jr. The Mother Superior remarked "see how mean these people are." With her third grade education from Italy she thought that the colored people had killed Dr. King. My quiet reaction was that it was my people that she was calling mean. Racial tensions were very high in Boston at this time. I had heard that the Ku Klux Klan, who I thought I had left in Louisiana, was having very successful rallies with the Irish in South Boston. When I rode through South Boston I could see why. I had never, ever seen such abject poverty. The reason I was told that there was so much racial unrest in South Boston was because of the poverty. The Irish people there blamed colored people for their poverty. They thought the coloreds were getting the jobs, the welfare, the opportunities that they could not get.

My plan was to die a happy nun. God had other plans for me. One evening I was kneeling alone in the chapel a few months before I was to take perpetual vows. A sad, sad feeling came over me and God was clearly telling me that it was time for me to leave the convent. The tears just rolled down my face when I realized that this is what God really wanted me to do. I argued with God. I said "God this is the only life I know." God insisted that it was time for me to go. It was as though I could feel the strong hand of God pushing me out of the door. The next day I told my superiors and they said "Oh no, you do not want to leave here. You would be like a fish out of water." I went back in prayer about it and the Lord said for me to get my airline ticket and leave. The nuns used a number of scare tactics to try to get me to stay. They almost convinced me that if I walked out of that door God was going to strike me dead. Also, they said I would be a big disappointment to my family. On the contrary I told them that my mother said if ever I wanted to leave she would send me a plane ticket. I was in a tug of war. I had to deal with God pushing me out of the door on the one hand and the nuns pulling me to stay on the other. I could not understand how God wanted me to leave a life I had comfortably settled into and given entirely over to him and venture out into the vast unknown. It was scary. God won the battle and when my temporary vows expired I left the convent. For a long time my family had wanted me to leave the convent. They said they were just waiting for me to come to my senses but I would not. They felt that the nuns had brainwashed me. For example, I needed some new nun shoes. I wrote and asked my mother to go to the Red Cross shoe store to purchase them and send them to me, which she did. It just so happened that my family came that summer to visit me in Boston. My mother saw that I had on some old beat up shoes and asked me what happened to the new shoes that she sent me? I cheerfully told her that Mother Superior got my new shoes and that I got Mother Superior's old shoes and that it was an honor for me to wear her old shoes because she is a saint. My parents were ready to drag me home then and there but my mother said to let me make up my own mind.

Once I left the convent and returned to the South, I encountered one big problem – a language barrier. I had acquired such a thick Boston accent that people could not understand what I was saying. Some of my relatives made fun of how I talked – caw for car, poc for park, doc for dark –don't poc your caw in the doc which translated meant "don't park your car in the dark. That's how I sounded. I realized right away that I had to practice getting a southern accent.

On my return home my parents were still very much involved in the NAACP. The NAACP was founded in 1909 by a group of white and African Americans who were outraged by accounts of lynchings. Its mission is to ensure the political, educational, social and economic equality of rights of all persons and to eliminate racial hatred and racial discrimination. Its name, retained in accordance with tradition, uses the once common term "colored people." At its founding the NAACP had only one African American on its board – Dr. W. E. B. Du Bois. It was predominantly white and heavily Jewish American.

I heard a lot of talk about how the colored soldiers at the Army base where my daddy worked were racially mistreated and how the town where the base was located was so racist that the white police department would beat up every young colored male they ever saw walking down the street and would sexually assault every young colored female. The cries got louder and my parents went to this town to take written complaints from the colored soldiers and the colored townspeople. They had permission to set up some temporary offices on the grounds of the Free Masons. All day they waited and only one person came from the small town. The Colonel at the base forbade the colored soldiers to leave the base. Towards the end of the day however, a multitude of police cars surrounded my parents and their companions and arrested them. When my mother saw them arresting my daddy she asked why were they arresting him? They told her that if she wanted to know why then she was also under arrest. Once she was in the police car she asked again why were they being arrested and they told her they would think of something. They were thrown into a jail with deplorable conditions. My mother got sick in a cell and my daddy could not help her because they were in separate locations in the jail. We waited all night for our parents to come home and finally the morning news said they were in jail. Anyone who went to the town to get them out of jail was also thrown in jail. Finally, word got to the governor of the state and he ordered the mayor and the police to let them out of jail.

Once my parents and their companions were out of that jail the NAACP called for a massive march on that town to bring attention to the injustices. Before the march the officials from that town sent two officials to tell my daddy that if he showed up in that town they would shoot him on sight. The day of the march came and my parents prepared to go to the march. I was fresh out of the convent and not too much into this but I decided that if my parents were going to die that day, I should go too. So I got on the bus with them and we headed for the little town. We just rode and waited for the bullets to start flying. What amazed me most was that we were easy targets because we rode in a school bus with windows all around. I watched my parents as we rode along. I detected no fear, no anxiety, nothing different from their normal selves. They had the same dispositions, same jokes, nothing different. They were willing to lay their lives on the line for justice and equality. I greatly honor them for their strength and courage.

I remember so many incredibly courageous people coming to our home. They risked their very lives going door-to-door registering African Americans to vote. I know people who have lost their jobs, their livelihoods, the only way they could provide bread on their table for their families because they stood up against employment discrimination. They are not perfect people, not saints but they risked it all for a vision of a more just society. They sacrificed to make it happen. One of my family's closest friends comes to mind. This gentleman was very well educated with a Master's Degree. In the 1960's and 1970's he spoke out clearly, intelligently and nonviolently against racial discrimination. He paid a very dear price. No one would hire him. Being highly industrious, he, his wife, and his children learned to live, in the middle of the city, off of the land. They would hunt and fish. It amazed me how they trained their children to survive even in the marshlands of southwest Louisiana. One of their sons is now a district judge but few people know that if you took him out deep, deep into snake and alligator infested marshlands and left him there, he could quickly find his way back, unharmed.

Once out of the convent I focused on getting my Bachelor's degree. I was a Junior in college but many colleges would not give me credit for all of my theology and church history courses. I went to the local university in my town for summer school. The racial tensions between the white and black students were overwhelming. We were not being called Negroes anymore. Neither were we being called coloreds. We were now saying it loud "I'm black and I'm proud."

I applied to a predominantly black Catholic university across the state and they accepted all of my credits. On the black Catholic campus I found a different kind of racial tension. It was between the black faculty members and the white faculty members. The black faculty members were accusing the white faculty members of inciting the black students to protests. I was never involved in any protests but I am forever grateful to my white professors, especially in American literature. They did an amazing job of teaching us to read and interpret black authors – Frederick Douglas, Ralph Ellison, Eldridge Cleaver, James Baldwin, Malcolm X, Dr. King and others.

The nuns were absolutely correct when they said I would be like a fish out of water. I became like someone who had been in captivity for a long period of time and needed to be deprogrammed. I was lost and I came to believe that I had been brainwashed.

So, I rebelled against everything I had ever been taught about God, about the church, the Sacraments, anything and everything that gave even the slightest hint of being connected with religion. I was now a free spirit, a free thinking adult, with new found freedom in the world. Look out world, here I come. Whatever I believed, until now, I was convinced, I believed because someone told me to do so. As the saying goes, I threw out the baby with the bath water and I began to believe in nothing. I could not even say the word "God' because that is what they told me to say. It was Karl Marx who said "Religion is the opium of the people." This was particularly true, I believed, of oppressed people. My mother would wake me up on Sunday mornings to go to Mass and I would say I have been to Mass enough to last me a lifetime. My only goal in life was to get an education otherwise life became totally meaningless to me. In Walden I Henry David Thoreau says: "The mass of men lead lives of quiet desperation." This desperation was very acceptable to me and I was just living like everybody else. It was all about surviving the rat race day after day and waiting to die. It was an empty, hollow existence that I lived for quite some time until one day after some serious introspection my free mind was telling me that I could believe in a higher power even though I could not call that higher power "God" because that was the word I had been told to use. Mostly it was the magnificence of nature and the orderliness and perfection of creation that brought me to accept this higher power. After a considerable amount of time and reflection I finally conceded to call the higher power "God." I thought it was a harmless concession especially since I needed to name the higher power and I could not think of a better name than "God." Much later I started to feel as though I was missing something because I did not believe in anything. I became determined to find the truth and believe in it with all of my heart and soul. That is what I was missing – not knowing the real truth. I needed to find out, no matter what it was. But, I did not want to believe in just any old thing. I wanted to say this is it. This is the truth. I found it. More importantly, I found it on my own.

In the convent we had studied so many different philosophies (even atheistic) along with logic, epistemology, and Metaphysics. I was an honor student in philosophy. Different philosophic theories about how we relate to the world outside of ourselves intrigued me. Perhaps I should live according to one of these philosophies, I thought. I went back and studied all of the major philosophers that we studied in the convent even the atheistic ones. This time was different, no one was telling me how to interpret or accept or reject what I studied. My free mind would determine what I should believe or not believe. One by one the philosophers fell. There were so many gaping loopholes in their theories that I could not bring myself to professing something I knew was in error.

One day it dawned on me that I should be Jewish. I loved the history of the Hebrew people and their relationship with God throughout the Hebrew Bible. The more I read the Old Testament the more I was convinced that I should become an Orthodox Jew. That is until I read the book of Isaiah. The Messianic prophesies in Isaiah presented a major obstacle to my becoming Jewish. It became obvious to me that the prophesies were referring to Jesus Christ and that they were fulfilled in Jesus Christ. Moreover, I concluded that Jesus Christ is the Messiah, the suffering savior of the world. Since Jews do not believe this I had to give up becoming Jewish. Once I admitted that Jesus Christ is the Savior, my free mind started to put the pieces of the puzzle together. I went back to the very beginning. God created incredibly superior beings – angelic creatures, all spirit, no bodies. At some point God revealed to these magnificent creatures that one day He would take on a human body and that they would have to fall down and worship a God-man. These angelic creatures were so far superior to humans that they refused to bow down to an inferior being. To them, for God to become man was such a come down and humiliation for God. One spiritual writer says that it would be like a human being, with intelligence and free will, entering into the body of a snake, crawling on his belly and eating dirt. They set themselves up as God's enemy, to do battle with God. Michael the Archangel led the battle of casting out Lucifer and his legions into the pool of eternal fire.

Satan turned against God and he was successful in getting Adam and Eve to turn against God. After Adam disobeyed God, he was hiding in the Garden of Eden when God came looking for him. God asked him why he was hiding and he said he was hiding because he was naked. One spiritual writer says that before their sin, Adam and Eve's souls shone brilliantly through their bodies. The light of God illumined their bodies so greatly that they never knew they were naked until sin blew out the light in their souls. The gates of paradise were shut tight against Adam and his kind. Adam's disobedience was a major slap in the face of God. Satan had the victory and the reign of Satan began. He established his rule upon the earth – a rule in direct contradiction to God's rule – which is why Cain could kill his brother Abel.

When Holy Mary, the new Eve, said to the angel Gabriel "I am the servant of the Lord. Let it be done to me as you say," Luke 1:38, it was the beginning of the end for Satan. Mary's words undo the words of the old Eve. The sinless virgin would give birth to the sinless Christ. The Immaculate Conception was a necessity. Holy Mary, Mother of God had to be sinless. The Savior came into the world to defeat sin so he could not be born of a creature who was ever under the control of sin or even slightly tainted by sin or Satan. Satan would then have had control over Christ. God's work of defeating sin and Satan had begun. Jesus came to defeat the order of Satan and restore the order of God. Jesus came to reverse what Satan had done.

Adam's sin had so infected and polluted our spiritual bloodline that innocent blood was the only antibiotic. Innocent blood had to be shed to wipe away the sin and the guilt. The innocent blood of Jesus washes away our sin and guilt.

I encountered Jesus as never before. I was like St. Paul on the road to Damascus. The scales began to fall from my eyes. Elizabeth Johnson states in *Consider Jesus:* "Something exceedingly good happens to people in their encounter with Jesus Christ. Fundamentally they are put right with God. Consequently they come to themselves, being restored to inner integrity, healed in body and spirit. Relationships with other people are also healed and peace becomes a real possibility. People experience a new lease on life pervaded with hope in the future, even if it be hope against hope." (4)

After accepting Jesus as the Savior, the awful truth dawned on me. I would now have to find a religion, the one that aligned itself faithfully with what Jesus taught while he was on this earth. I went back, with my free mind, to study all of the major religions of the world, except Roman Catholicism. I already had enough of studying that one. One by one the religions began to fall. There was always some gaping issue that did not line up with what Jesus taught. Worse yet, most of them had broken off from Roman Catholicism over some moral or theological disagreements. The most awful thought of all occurred to me. I only had Roman Catholicism left. No problem, I thought, I can shoot that one full of holes. My free mind thoroughly analyzed all of the teachings of the Roman Catholic Church. I searched and searched all of the doctrines and moral teachings, everything. The more I studied, the more I could align the doctrines with what Jesus taught. When I completed my analysis, I was amazed at what my free mind was telling me – the Roman Catholic religion is the one true religion of Jesus Christ. WOW! The nuns had it right. God brought me full circle back to the religion of my baptism. But God gave me a very ecumenical lesson. The Holy Spirit hit me over the head with a brick to say that I had been sincere in my search for the truth and this is where it led me. There are other people who are just as sincere and there faith journey might lead them somewhere else and I must respect that. "Sincere" became the operative word for me. Once I realized that I had found my spiritual identity again in the Roman Catholic Church I committed myself to being a true Catholic. I promised God I would give it 200%. I returned to Mass and the Sacraments. Not even in the convent with years of prayer and meditation did I experience so much peace and joy as when I found God again in the Church. A short time after this experience I visited my home town church where I was baptized, made my First Communion and Confirmation. When I walked in the church that Sunday the choir was singing "Take me back, take me back dear Lord to the place where I first received you. Take me back, take me back dear Lord where I first believed." The tears rolled down my face and I praised God for bringing me out of the wilderness, out of the dark night of the soul and into his marvelous light.

CHAPTER 3

In His Image

"Then God Said: "Let us make man in
our image, after our likeness."
Genesis 1:26

I met my future husband, Glenn, while we were at the university and after I graduated we had a big New Orleans wedding. God gave Glenn to me and me to Glenn in life, in love and for all eternity.

After my graduation we lived in New Orleans and I taught at an all black Catholic elementary school. I was an excellent teacher and worked hard for my students to learn but my heart was not in it. The following year I signed a contract with an all girl Catholic High School. Again, I worked very hard and my students learned, but my heart was not in it. My professors had told me that I would make a good teacher. I thought they knew what they were talking about. Even though I was a dedicated teacher I felt like a square peg trying to fit into a round hole. I was trying to be who other people thought I should be. I then realized that my strength is in relating to adults.

Through an employment agency I applied for a job in journalism. The agency sent me on an interview at a major bank to apply for the position of proofreader in their new Word Processing Center. Basically they had computerized and centralized all correspondence going out of the bank and I was hired to proofread all correspondence going out of the typing pool. This bank is located in the heart of New Orleans and I had heard about how they did not like to hire black people. The word on the street was that they were so prejudiced that they would not even hire black elevator operators. It became a joke and people would ask why not, it does not require a whole lot of skills to operate an elevator. All you have to do is push the button. But this bank did not want its rich white uptown customers to even see a black elevator operator let alone a black teller. I think I was hired because I am a light-skinned black person and they have to meet certain EEOC minority quotas. However, it has been my experience that people who hate black people hate all shades of black.

The manager of the Word Processing Center decided to move to Florida. Because I played a major part in establishing the department's policies and procedures I assumed that I should be promoted to the manager's position. The Vice President over the department could not understand why I should think such a thing. I had to be very persistent in demanding that position and I got it. I did the hiring and the firing for the department. I hired people based strictly on their skills and work ethic. I hired some white people and some black people. Some of the white secretaries complained to my boss that I was hiring too many black people. He promised them that he would not let me hire anymore black people. Along comes a qualified black person for the job opening. I hired her and sent her papers to the Personnel Department to be processed. My supervisor stopped the process because he said she lied on her application by saying that she had lived in Boston, Massachusetts. I told him that that was not so because I had lived in Boston, Massachusetts and we discussed many things that only a person who lived there would know. I suggested that there was no reason not to hire her. He told me that if I insisted on hiring her that I would be demoted to another position in the bank. I was not about to back down from what I knew was right. I was sent to work as a technical writer in the Marketing Department. My job was to put together a multi-volume set of training manuals that would help tellers understand how to operate the new computerized teller system. I put my heart and soul into those manuals and the end result was an impressive seven volume set. Even foreign tellers said they were so clearly written that they could understand how to do their jobs. I later learned that a major technology company bought the rights to those manuals and marketed them in three different languages. As for me, the department took me to dinner at a French Quarter restaurant. I asked my supervisor if I should get a bonus or something for producing those manuals. He said "NO, it is just like if you were a chemist working for Dupont Chemical and you discover a new chemical. You don's get credit for it, the company does." I was very shocked and disappointed. I was dumb enough to believe in the American dream: "Work hard and you'll get ahead." Hard work got me nowhere. I kept running into, not a glass ceiling (at least glass can shatter) a concrete ceiling. When I left that bank I promised myself I would never, ever work for white people again.

Following my experiences at the bank I put a great deal of time and effort in trying to understand racism. It was a devastating experience. It was the first time that someone looked at me and I could feel hate radiating from them – just oozing out of their pores and I wanted to understand why.

On a spiritual level I knew that God's nature is reflected in every human being. We all bear the mark of God. Without exception we are his handiwork. When we look into the face of another human being whether it is a black face, brown face, red face, white face, yellow face or whatever, God is looking back at us, whether we like it or not.

To despise another human being based on their skin color grievously offends God. It insults God. It says that the hater does not like how God looks because he is a different color and has different features. He/she might have large lips or a large nose or nappy hair. This says to God that he created imperfection that he created someone that the hater finds not esthetically pleasing. God does not make mistakes and God does not create imperfection.

The system of slavery has left permanent marks on this nation. It was so profoundly diabolical. In his book *Erasing Racism: The Survival of the American Nation* Molefi Kete Asante, chillingly describes slavery: "Slavery was not a romantic system, it was evil, ferocious, brutal, and corrupting in all of its aspects. It was developed in its greatest degree of degradation in the United States. The enslaved African was treated with utter disrespect. No laws protected the African from any cruelty the white master could conceive. The man, woman, or child was at the complete mercy of the most brutish of people. For looking a white man in the eye, the enslaved person could have her eyes blinded with hot irons. For speaking up in defense of a wife or a woman, a man could have his right hand severed. For defending his right to speak against oppression, an African could have his tongue cut out. For running away and being caught, an enslaved African could have her Achilles tendon cut. For resisting the advances of her white master, a woman could be given fifty lashes of the cowhide whip. A woman who physically fought against her master's sexual advances was courting death, and many died at the hands of their masters. The enslaved African was more often than not physically scarred, crippled, or injured because of some brutal act of the slave owner. Among the punishments that were favored by the slave owners were whipping holes, where the enslaved was buried in the ground up to the neck, dragging blocks that were attached to the feet of men or women who had run away and been caught..." Historical accounts of the extreme brutality of slavery boggles the mind and insults our sensibilities. It is mind boggling to think that any human being could inflict such atrocities upon another human being.

Once slavery was illegal, the brutality turned into racism.

The *American Heritage College Dictionary* defines racism as "the belief that race accounts for differences in human character or ability and that a particular race is superior to others." Other definitions state that: "Racism is discrimination or prejudice based on race," and: "A group or population of humans categorized on the basis of various sets of heritable characteristics (such as color of skin, eyes and hair)." Searching further I discovered that race is a category invented by society. That's right, race is strictly man-made. God did not put race in our DNA (Deoxyribose Nucleic Acid) for us to be separated by skin color. Nearly all reputable geneticists agree that DNA cannot identify a person's race. God did not put it in our genetic makeup. Why? Because the color of a person's skin should not matter. All God wants us to see in another human being is a noble soul made in the image and likeness of God and saved by the blood of Jesus.

Eduardo Bonilla-Silva in his book *White Supremacy & Racism in the Post-Civil Rights Era* does incredibly extensive and erudite research on racism. He says; "Racism is prejudice, ignorance, or a disease that afflicts some individuals and causes them to discriminate against others just because of the way they look." He further states: "...the persistent inequality experienced by blacks and other racial minorities in the United States today is due to the *continued* albeit *changed* existence of a racial structure. In contrast to race relations in the Jim Crow period, however, racial practices that reproduce racial inequality in contemporary America are (1) increasingly covert, (2) embedded in normal operations of institutions, (3) void of direct racial terminology, and (4) invisible to most whites."

Satan uses every trick in the book to drag souls into hell. One of his greatest inventions is racism – despising another human being because of the color of their skin. It is right, straight out of the hands of the prince of evil. What my DNA research shows is that there are no pure populations. To some extent, most of the populations of the Americas is mixed. Mixed means that virtually all African Americans have some European DNA admixture. About one-third of white Americans show detectable African admixture. All Latin Americans are blended in proportions matching each region's colonial population.

Further my research showed that very often an American who looks white and is seen as white actually has significant African DNA and one who looks black and is seen as black has more than half European DNA. Many times my mother and I have been mistaken for white while we are Americans who are proud of our African ancestry.

I recall my mother telling me about her experiences as an OB-GYN nurse at the Air Force base hospital. She said the way they knew if a newborn was white or had Negro blood was by a grey circle on the baby's behind. If the baby had the circle they were Negro. However, she said there were many babies with the circle who were listed as Caucasian because their parents were listed as Caucasian. This grey spot is known as the Mongolian blue spot which commonly occurs among dark skinned people. Most East Asians, East Africans and people descended from Native Americans carry the mark when born.

I have heard so many stories about Negroes who passed for white. They did not want to be identified with an oppressed people. Some of them were found out and suffered the consequences. One of our school mates decided to pass for white. She moved to California and married a white man. Eventually he found out that she was Negro, beat her up and kicked her out. Many, many others have never been found out.

The U. S. Census Bureau is in a real quandary about how to count millions and millions of Americans who are racially mixed and do not know how to classify themselves. There has been a huge rise in the number of racially mixed Americans. This is largely due to racially mixed children born in the 1970's, 80's, and 90's. Experts predict that the U. S. is moving towards becoming a brown majority race. They call it the browning of America and it is happening rapidly.

As a light-skinned African American woman, I have a unique perspective on race. My tall, dark and very handsome husband and I were frequently mistaken for an interracial couple. We got stared down in restaurants and other places. How profoundly ignorant to judge by appearances, not knowing we were both of the same race.

Maybe because I grew up in a strong civil rights family I personally have never reaped any "benefits" from being light-skinned. I have heard that there are "perks" for light-skinned black people. Being an outspoken civil rights advocate caused me to miss out on the "perks." The same is true for my mother who looked so white but she was so militant. I am sure that she also missed out on the "benefits."

One night my parents were traveling back home by car from a civil rights meeting in another town. It was getting real late and they were too tired to continue driving. They decided to spend the night at a nearby hotel. They spotted a hotel that did not have any cars and pulled into the parking lot. My daddy went into the hotel lobby to register while my mother was gathering their belongings in the car. When my daddy went to the registration desk the desk clerk told him that they did not have any vacant rooms. My daddy was surprised and asked how could that be since there were no cars in the parking lot and no one in the lobby? The clerk insisted that they had no vacancies. My daddy went out to the car to tell my mother but she was too tired to accept this. So she went to the desk while my daddy sat in the car. The desk clerk was checking my mother into a room when my daddy showed up in the lobby with their luggage. He said he figured she must be getting a room since she took so long. The desk clerk was very annoyed with him when he looked up and saw him bringing in his luggage. He told my daddy that he had already told him that they did not have any vacant rooms. My daddy told him: "If my wife is staying here I certainly am too." Needless to say, they put both of them out. My daddy reported this to the FBI (Federal Bureau of Investigation). A few days later they called him back to say that the hotel in question would now be very happy if he and his wife would stay there the next time they are in town.

I have heard many, many stories about how civil rights workers never wanted to be caught in small southern towns after dark. Even if their car broke down or ran out of gas they would keep walking rather than stop after dark in one of these towns.

I well recall a white ladies club wanting my mother to join their club and she was interested in joining. One of the ladies told my mother that she would come to her home to speak to her about the club. When the lady came to the house my dark skin sister answered the door and told her that she was not at home. Later the white lady club member called my mother and told her that she had come to her house and that her maid had told her that she was not home. In surprise my mother said: "My maid, that was not my maid that was my daughter!" Needless to say they no longer wanted my mother in the club.

Many times in stores, even to this very day, a white salesperson or cashier thinks that I am a white person. They are so warm and friendly as long as they think this. Once I say or do something for them to know that I am not white their whole attitude changes. Immediately they become cold and unfriendly and look at me like I suddenly grew horns.

How profoundly ignorant of some black people who fell into self-hatred and discriminate against their own race. In New Orleans I heard of the black social club, years ago, that had a brown bag test for admittance. This meant that if the person's skin was darker than a brown paper bag they were not admitted. We should not be surprised that some poor, ignorant black slaves bought into white supremacy. Slavery taught the slaves that everything African was bad. Their descendants have been bombarded with this. Even in the old black and white cowboy movies the good guy wore a white hat and the bad guy wore a black hat.

The media has, for decades, etched negative images of African Americans in the minds of the general public. These negative images are so strong that it has negatively impacted the self-esteem of individual African Americans and the overall view of an entire race of people. Many African Americans believe that this began with the old Amos and Andy Show portraying African Americans as less intelligent than other races, lazy, fearful, shuffling and grinning. This was followed by Aunt Jemima, then Julia, a black nurse with a son and no husband. Television still has great difficulty depicting the African American family with a father, mother and children. Until Good Times, which was in a housing project, I do not recall any two-parent African American families on television.

Later we have Bill Cosby and the Huxtables who are too rich and successful for most African American families to relate to. Whenever welfare is mentioned on the evening news, a black face is flashed on the screen even though it is statistically true that more white Americans are on welfare in this country than African Americans. According to the evening news and newspapers you would think that most young African Americans are hanging out on street corners, doing drugs, robbing or raping people, or in prison. The images are so damaging that research has shown that when little African American girls are given a choice between playing with an African American doll or a white doll, they overwhelmingly choose the white doll. It is extremely difficult for African Americans to assert their self-esteem and self-worth when systemic negativism is so prevalent in the media.

Some white people like to say that African tribesmen sold their own people into slavery. I think this is historically true. They think that this gets them off of the hook and that we should deal with racism among ourselves and leave them alone. We are dealing with it among ourselves. To this day we are doing everything in our power to combat black on black crime but this is no excuse for their white supremacy attitude and behavior.

In my search for the root causes of racism, I took some time to read over many of the black authors we studied in college such as Ralph Ellison *The Invisible Man*. Society does not see him because he is black, he is a non-person. This greatly intrigued me. How can anyone be a non-person? The fact that he exists gives him personhood but hate has stripped him of his personhood.

The more I read about the black experience, the more I was horrified by man's inhumanity to man. Most horrific was the history of lynchings. The year was 1912 in Cordele, Georgia. Eighteen year old Albert Hamilton was a young black man who made a living driving horse-drawn carriages. He was accused (true or otherwise) of assaulting a white woman. He was carried off to jail. Later, a mob dragged him from his cell, beat him severely, hanged him from a nearby tree and shot him more than 300 times. According to statistics, between 1880 and 1940, over 5,000 African Americans were lynched in the United States. That number is not so accurate because some small towns never reported the number of their lynchings. Lynchings have been called the Negro Holocaust.

There are accounts of "postcard lynchings" where pictures were taken and postcards were sold. Some whites were lynched during this time but blacks were the main targets of sadistic mobs employing burning, torture and dismemberment to prolong suffering and excite a "festive atmosphere" among the killers and onlookers. White families would bring their small children to watch, newspapers some times carried advance notices, railroad agents sold excursion tickets to announced lynching sites, and mobs cut off black victims' fingers, toes, ears, or genitalia as souvenirs. The mob was the judge, the jury and the executioner. It has also been proven that a good number of the blacks who were lynched were falsely accused. Lynching was an institutionalized method used by whites to terrorize African Americans and maintain white supremacy.

Numerous, incredibly horrible accounts of injustices and murder after murder of blacks are an ugly part of American history. Some lynchings were so gruesome that the details will make you sick to the stomach. But if you can stomach it, read what happened to Claude Neal in Florida in 1934 (in biography of Harry Moore, entitled "Before His Time"). The details are so ugly and shocking editors would not print it in the paper. Neal's body also, ended up on a postcard, selling for 50 cents each. No one was ever brought to justice for these brutal murders. In many cases, the law helped to commit the murders. The treatment of blacks was so cruel and insane that the victims were not even considered victims.

Abel Meeropol expressed his horror at lynchings in his poem *Strange Fruit.* In 1939 Billie Holiday composed the music and lyrics to this poem. This has to be one of the most powerful poems ever written in the English language. The strange fruit hanging from the poplar trees were black bodies.

For many years, southern senators blocked anti-lynching legislation. However, it is well documented that white people, especially white women's groups helped to abolish lynchings. Recently the Congress offered an apology to all African Americans for this "Negro Holocaust."

I know many white people who say "that was then, this is now, get over it." Not so, not so fast, as a matter of fact I have come to accept this response as very racially charged. I call this the Pontius Pilate complex. They want to wash their hands of all guilt. My question is: "do you tell the Jews to get over the holocaust?" In 2007 nooses were hung from a tree at a school in Jena, Louisiana.

Slavery is dead. It is unlawful to buy, sell or torture people in this country. Slavery is dead but its offspring white supremacy is alive and well. It is this offspring which causes long term racial inequalities and injustices.

The story of James Byrd, Jr. shocked the nation and the world. On June 7, 1998 in Jasper, Texas, three men, consumed by racial hatred, chained James Byrd, Jr. to the back of a pickup truck and dragged him to his death. He was torn limb from limb. In a larger sense, this is always the result of hate. It tears us apart. In the wake of the devastating effects of hatred, a few stark realities might creep into our consciousness. Then we say it is time to put it all behind us and heal. This seems to be the acceptable response. To me, the problem with this response is that we avoid dealing with the root causes of hatred and no one ever really heals.

One of the stark realities that the horrible murder of James Byrd, Jr. should cause us to face is that many white Americans mistakenly cast racism as the sin of their parents or grandparents. They even congratulate themselves for moving beyond the mistakes of the past. They have a lot of difficulty understanding why African Americans concern themselves with civil rights or continue to push for affirmative action. It is a huge deception to believe racism was wiped out with the civil-rights legislation of the 60's. To effectively deal with any disorder we must first cease denying that the disorder exists. When reality hits us smack in the face, as in Jasper, it should be a rallying point for us to positively take action against violence and hate in our society. The usual, meaningless, superficial gestures only serve to perpetuate the legacy of racism. One week after the murder of James Byrd, Jr. the headlines read that the furor was over in Jasper and that the people were beginning to put the incident behind them. This is why we never really heal and why Jasper will never really heal, precisely because the furor is over. We forget so easily, we want to forget horror and hate. This selective and repressive memory enables us to continue to reap the fruits of injustice, racial misunderstanding, massive mistrust and fear that paralyzes whole communities. As long as white

Americans and African Americans continue to sweep racial hatred under the rug, history will continue to repeat itself.

I recall comments made by Camille Cosby, wife of famed comedian Bill Cosby, regarding the man who killed her only son. She said: "Society taught him to hate." If we accept the premise that hate is learned and taught, then we can assume that to eradicate hate it must be unlearned and untaught. Camille Cosby had struggled with understanding what human conditions or dispositions would produce such enormous hatred resulting in robbing her son of his very life.

In my opinion, slavery never died. It just changed outfits, put on a different face but the mind and the heart never changed. During slavery times white folks thought that they were superior to African Americans. Today white folks still think they are superior to African Americans. What changed? The law forbids slavery so they come up with other laws to perpetuate their superiority – Jim Crow laws and voter suppression laws and more. – same old song, different verse.

Bryan P. Stone in his book *Compassionate Ministry* says that we must deal with the deformation of community that racism has inflicted upon our culture. It is a national malignant cancer for which we must never cease to find a cure. Stone gives some insight into the first step of healing when he quotes Jim Wallis: "All white people in the United States have benefited from the structure of racism, whether or not they even committed a racist act, uttered a racist word, or had a racist thought (as unlikely as that is). Just as surely as blacks suffer in a white society because they are black, whites benefit because they are white. And since whites have profited from a racist structure, whites must try to change it."

I have said repeatedly that government has over studied the oppressed. We know everything there is to know about the oppressed. It is long past time that we focus on the oppressor and upon freeing the oppressor from his "peculiar demons" as James Cone calls them in *Compassionate Ministry*. I have never known racism to be the fault of the victim.

White supremacy is the disorder. The oppressor needs liberating. Unfortunately, if white America continues to be in denial about this, there is no healing.

While researching and studying these things, I wrote this short poem:

The Statue of Liberty

The Statue of Liberty a mockery indeed.
Give me your tired, your poor, those in need.
Unfit mother to the black child of your womb –
loving other's children more than your own.
Your torch looms high in vengeful skies.
It gives no warmth, no light – a torch of stone.

CHAPTER 4

Life on the New Plantation

"You have been told, O man, what is good, and what the Lord requires of you; only to do the right and to love goodness, and to walk humbly with your God." Micah 6:8

Here we are in 2013 America marking the 50th Anniversary of the March on Washington and Dr. King's very famous "I have a dream" speech. On the steps of the Lincoln Memorial in Washington, D. C. August 28, 1963 he said: "I have a dream that my four little children will one day live in a nation where they will not be judged by the colour of their skin but by the content of their character." We stop to reflect upon whether the dream has become a reality in the past fifty years? The truth is that in some ways it has and in other ways it has turned into a reoccurring nightmare.

Now we are called African Americans which I think is very appropriate. We are red-blooded Americans, born and raised in this country, of African ancestry. We are just as American as Polish Americans or Irish Americans or German Americans. This is our country, our native land.

According to the latest National Urban League Report the percentage of African Americans living in poverty declined 23 points. The percentage of African Americans completing high school has greatly improved along with the number of African Americans enrolled in colleges and graduating from colleges.

The percentage of African Americans living in poverty, the percentage of African American children living in poverty and the percentage of African Americans who own their homes show significant progress.

Hardly any progress has been made in closing the African American-white income gap and the unemployment gap. These have become reoccurring nightmares. Great racial disparities still exist in education, housing, employment and the criminal justice system. White Americans have the opportunities to achieve the American dream, African Americans do not. There is no level playing field. African Americans who do succeed generally do so against great odds. There are many misguided, feverish attempts to outlaw Affirmative Action so that the playing field will never be leveled. Quite a few cases are before the Supreme Court alleging reverse discrimination which I think is an oxymoron. It is absurd to think that white people could possibly sincerely believe that they have any disadvantages in a full blown racist system that has been, and still is, skewed against black Americans. I compare this to a pie, a great, big pie. White America has the whole pie, sliced up. I, black America, ask for a piece of the pie. White America says no because it will mean less pie for white America. I say to white America "but you have the whole pie and all of the other pieces, I only want a piece." White America still says "No." If somehow laws are enacted to help me get a piece of that pie they cry reverse discrimination.

The greatest achievement in the last fifty years has to be the election of President Barack Obama as the first African American President of the United States of America. He was born on August 4, 1961 in Hawaii of a black father and a white mother. He is the great American success story – middle class upbringing with strong family values. He is a Harvard Law School graduate and the first African American President of the *Harvard Law Review.* Later he taught constitutional law at the University of Chicago and served in the Illinois State Senate. When he was elected the 44th President of the United States on November 4, 2008 we were a proud nation. Maybe not all of us but the great majority of African Americans, Latinos, college students, and women who turned out to vote in the first African American president could savor an historical moment. He even won the Catholic vote. One group he did not win was the white male vote. Some editorials call them "angry" white males. They could not and still do not accept an African American being president of the United States of America and leader of the free world. I do not think that there has ever been any president in the history of this country who has received more death threats than President Obama. With the election of President Obama racial hatred skyrocketed. The haters are out full force. I personally overheard a white man say that he could not understand why someone has not as yet put a bullet in Obama's head. The hate in him was so strong that he did not care who heard. I call this racism out loud and it is very loud.

The issue persisted about whether or not President Obama was born in the United States and is an American citizen. Even after he produced his birth certificate some still do not accept it. There is still a wide spread false rumor that he is a Muslim. I have seen and heard President Obama, on national television, professing his faith in Jesus Christ.

It is a well known fact that President Obama inherited an economic nightmare from former President George W. Bush. He had to hit the ground running to keep this country from going off the fiscal cliff. He made the gutsy decision to go after the world's greatest terrorist, Osama Bin Laden, responsible for the 9/11 attacks, when President Bush had given up. He had many achievements in his first term and shocked the haters by being convincingly reelected in November 2012 for a second term. It was at this time that a group of conservative Republicans vowed to block any and everything that he would try to do. What a sad day for the people of this country! Lawmakers abdicating their responsibilities to the people and to the nation in order to tear down the president. Anti-Obama sentiment runs high throughout this country. Some say they oppose him because they have differing political views or different ideologies. The bottom line is the majority of people who oppose him do so because he is African American. There is one cable network that spews out anti-Obama venom seven days a week 24/7. There are people who listen and watch this day after day until their minds are exhausted with anti-Obama rhetoric. Not only does it flood the conservative radio and television air waves some are even preaching it in their churches. They go to extremes to demonize and disrespect President Obama. They want to make him out to be the anti-Christ. There is not a shred of truth in what they say. They are driven by hate.

Politically I classify myself as a conservative Democrat. I am a staunch pro-life Catholic. I believe in the sacredness of life from the cradle to the grave. As strongly as I oppose abortion I also oppose capitol punishment. I fully accept and support the teachings of the Catholic Church on contraception, same-sex marriages and homosexuality. However, I am firmly convinced that Jesus would not be a Republican.

One Republican lawmaker produced a budget that was so offensive to the poor and middle class of the country that he was chided by the U.S. Conference of Catholic Bishops. A Jesuit priest remarked about that budget: "Survival of the fittest may be ok for social Darwinists but not for followers of the gospel of compassion and love." The extreme bias that Republicans have for the rich is in stark contrast to the teachings of Jesus Christ. It demonizes the poor – robs from the poor and middle class to give to the rich. They want to cut or eliminate Social Security and Medicare and other safety net programs. They falsely claim that by cutting out food stamps it will make people get a job. This completely ignore the fact that a large number of people on food stamps already work. They are called the working poor. How can they get jobs when the Republicans voted against President Obama's jobs program? How can children get jobs, or the elderly or the disabled who are receiving food stamps?

It is a fact that the majority of poor people in this country are white people. While a disproportionate number are non-white. Typically Republicans use budget cuts to signal to their base that they are getting welfare queens and lazy blacks off of government dependency. People of all stripes are dying everyday because they cannot afford health care. President Obama proposed a national health care plan to help these people and the Republicans live to tear it down. Ironically, much of the Affordable Care Act or "Obamacare" is based on Republican ideas. They do not want to tear down Obamacare. They want to tear down Obama. President Obama says that he does not mind that it is called "Obamacare" because he does care.

Then there is the hysteria over losing our religious liberties because of some Department of Health and Human Services provisions regarding who pays for contraceptives for employees. Churches are exempt from this provision. The furor was mostly at Catholic hospitals and universities. It seems to me that some religious leaders have become so worldly that they have compromised their religious principles. If religious institutions cannot run without federal dollars they have put themselves in a very compromising position. Instead of finding ways to break the addiction I have heard priests railing against "Obamacare" from the altar. I offer a very basic, simple solution to the conflict between DHHS and religious institutions. The obvious solution is for religious institutions not to take the money. For example, 70 percent of the funding for Catholic Relief Services comes from the U.S. government. The question is, have religious institutions become so addicted to federal funds that they have abdicated their own religious freedom? "If you dance to the music, you must pay the piper" as the saying goes. Religious institutions would need to wean themselves off of the federal gravy train to be free to deal with contraceptives, adoptions, foster care and immigration according to their consciences. We cannot have our cake and eat it too. Proverbs 15:16: "Better a little with fear of the Lord than a great fortune with anxiety."

Herein lies the wisdom of the separation of church and state. The state is interested in civil liberties, that everyone is treated the same, whether pro-choice, pro-life or pro-gay marriage. Whatever rights are afforded to one must be afforded to all. This can be legislated. The church is concerned with the spiritual formation of the faithful and saving souls, with God's law and morality which cannot be legislated. Because the constitution states that no national religion shall be established, I cannot demand that the government outlaw contraceptives. It also clearly states that the government shall not make laws that violate my religious beliefs. However, all of my life I have been opposed to capitol punishment but the government does not care a hill of beans about my religious belief. God's law and man-made laws are frequently in conflict.

One young priest, from the altar, compared the health care issue to that of St. Thomas Moore in England in 1534 who was beheaded for defying King Henry VIII. He portrayed our religious freedom as so threatened that the government storm troopers are coming soon to drag us out of our homes and cut off our heads if we do not do what the government says. The religious right war drums are beating loud in defense of religious liberty, demonizing President Obama and "Obamacare." What is wrong with this picture? God is God over the church and God over the state. God does not want his church so entangled with the state that they become confused about the dividing lines. Jesus drew a hard line in the sand when he said: "Then render to Ceasar the things that are Ceasar's and to God the things that are God's." Matthew 22:21

Since the church is in the business of saving souls, they should have informed their flock about the evils of contraceptives, abortion and homosexuality. If they are true shepherds after the heart of Jesus Christ their main concern would be to assure that every member of their flock knows what is a sin and what is sinful behavior. As long as members of their flock are not demanding contraceptives, abortions and engaging in homosexual activities they are doing their ministry to help save souls. Eliminating the demand among their flock should be their concern. Statistics show that a high percentage of Catholic women used or use contraceptives. They evidently were or are not well informed about the teachings of the church in this regard. The government is not the problem. The government is not going to explain sin or the difference between good and evil to these women. That is the responsibility of the church. No matter what laws the government makes it all comes down to a lone woman walking into a pharmacy or an abortion clinic and making a decision.

I wrestled with the question of how to vote on the abortion issue. So I went to discuss it with my spiritual advisor – the holiest priest I have ever known. I told him about my struggle with wanting to protect the unborn but at the same time I could not vote for people who support capitol punishment or make laws that hurt the poor and middle class. He told me very clearly that there are some people who only care about life in the womb but they do not care about life once it gets here.

I firmly believe that our pro-life voices must be heard over the pro-choice voices. All of us who choose life must be heard. This is not a Democratic issue, or Republican issue or liberal or conservative issue; this is a matter of life or death.

Whatever else this nation might accomplish means absolutely nothing as long as the blood of the innocents continues to be shed. What good is it to guarantee every citizen the right to life, liberty and the pursuit of happiness, give every able-bodied citizen a good paying job; put a chicken in every pot; wipe out racism, discrimination, drug abuse and wars; yet refuse to recognize the rights of the unborn? What good is it to be the greatest nation on earth while the blood of the innocents is dripping from our national hands?

I do not engage in scientific debates about when life begins. I do know that a very living, moving sperm, meets up with a very living egg and they form a new life. In fact, they had to be living to form new life. I believe that the fertilized human ovum has an absolute right to life. God is in the business of breathing life and God does not play to science. Science is for the service of God. Who is alive today who does not live by the breath of God? Moreover, we were in the mind of God even before the sperm fertilized the egg as sacred scripture states in the appointment of Jeremiah as a prophet "Before I formed you in the womb I knew you, and before you were born, I consecrated you." Jeremiah 1:4-5. Psalm 139:13-16 refers to God's creation of human life as follows: "For you created my inmost being; you knit me together in my mother's womb." Who is so bold as to second-guess God? Who is so arrogant as to presume that God makes mistakes? Who is so bold as to snuff out the very breath of God and to slap God's hands while he is knitting life in the womb? Who is so bold? The United States of America, that's who. The United States of America has one of the highest abortion rates in the developed world. Abortion crosses every socioeconomic, racial, ethnic, religious and age group. The majority of these abortions occur because the child is unwanted or inconvenient. Abortionists mitigate the rights of the unborn by claiming alleged benefits to others.

Years ago minority women could not afford abortions. So their white sisters decided to help these disadvantaged women to have the resources to kill their babies too. Now minority women have abortions at an alarming rate. The slaves would celebrate in the fields when a baby was born especially a son, whom they hoped God might anoint as a new Moses and their deliverer. They rejoiced when they were able to carry their babies to full term. Financially they had absolutely nothing but it did not cross their minds that they could not afford to have babies. They survived under the most brutal of circumstances. How can a people become a majority if the women are killing their babies? For black women abortion seems like a cruel joke. Not too long ago there was a national outcry about how many black babies were on welfare. Now we cannot be consoled in our loud lamentations as we count how many will never live.

I had to ask myself: "Would Jesus vote Republican?" The answer is "No." "Then they will answer and say, 'Lord, when did we see you hungry or thirsty or a stranger or naked or ill or in prison, and not minister to your needs?' He will answer them, 'Amen, I say to you, what you did not do for one of these least ones, you did not do for me'." Matthew 25:44-46.

One of the chief complaints that conservative Republicans say they have against President Obama is that he wants to expand the powers of government and spend a lot of money having government do for people what they can do for themselves. They do not believe that government has any obligations to the people (only to rich people). They believe that government should not be providing food stamps or housing assistance or a head start for children or educational assistance for college students. It makes you wonder just who is the real anti-Christ? Shame, shame, shame on this nation, or any nation, with no heart, no compassion, no outreach to the people crying out to God for a decent living for themselves and their children.

Nationally and locally schools are separated by race. Housing is separated by race. Employment is profoundly impacted by race. Some churches are separated by race. Racism is everywhere – in the very air we breathe.

Regarding education I once heard Dick Gregory say that white folks say that education is our problem. Then he asks if we are aware that in 1950 Dr. Charles

Drew, a black doctor, who invented blood plasma bled to death in the front of a North Carolina hospital because white doctors refused to admit him? There are many well educated African Americans and they experience a covert, subtle form of racism. They either must act white and accept whatever crumbs fall from the master's table or accept being unemployed or underemployed. This proves to me that education was never our problem – white supremacy is the problem.

Once a year in the month of May we commemorate the Supreme Court decision of Brown verses the Board of Education of Topeka, Kansas. The Brown decision in 1954 declared separate but equal, as espoused in the Plessy v. Ferguson decision to be unconstitutional. So 59 years later that means that most, if not all, of our education systems are unconstitutional, as they are more and more racially segregated. We know that this is mainly the result of racially segregated neighborhoods. When an African American family moves into a white neighborhood, the white families move out, sending their children to schools in other parts of town. This creates one-race schools.

Generally, the best teachers are at the white schools, which is why test scores are generally lower in African

American schools. Racial disparities in education are pervasive and rapidly growing across the nation. There is an over representation of African American students in special education and an under representation in gifted and talented courses. There are disparities in access to early childhood education, disparities in suspensions and expulsions, and disparities in graduation rates, to name a few.

I am opposed to school vouchers and charter schools. They take much needed resources from the public school system. As a civil rights activist I view vouchers and charter schools as back door segregation. They do not solve anything. They compound the problem. The solution is not to give the child a voucher to get out of a low scoring school, but to raise the scores of the school. Now that takes a lot of work and a lot of money. The solution is not to say that the child will learn better in a separate charter school. Sooner or later that child will have to face the problems and racial diversity of the real world that they left.

My study of black history taught me to strongly oppose one-race schools, be they black or white. Seeing so many film-clips of dogs and hoses being used on black students trying to get an equal education at all white schools taught me this. I also learned that even if a one race school, white or black has an excellent academic rating, it is fundamentally offering substandard exclusive education by denying its participants the benefits of diverse interactions with other races. This negatively impacts white and black students.

It is not necessary for African American children to sit in a classroom next to white children in order to learn. What is necessary is for African American children to have a fighting chance by having access to the same quality teachers, the same quality books, the same quality educational programs and scholarships.

In my small town we have upscale neighborhoods with expensive homes and well manicured lawns. They were once all white neighborhoods. Now, all of them are owned and maintained by African Americans – physicians, attorneys, educators and other professionals. The homes and the lawns are still very well kept and as beautiful as ever. When the African American families moved in the neighborhood, the white families moved out. Many white Americans still refuse to live in a neighborhood with African Americans. Their original plan was to price all African

Americans out of the neighborhood but in some cases some African Americans made enough money to buy in. Even though redlining of property is illegal, realtors know how to get around steering African Americans to live in African American neighborhoods and whites to live in white neighborhoods.

Loan discrimination and insurance discrimination are still wide spread and very subtle.

It would take another book to analyze all of the inequalities and injustices in the criminal justice system. One black comedian joked about it when he said that he went down to the court house seeking justice and that is what he found **just us**. It is hard to laugh at a system that we trust to be the epitome of fairness and justice being riddled through and through with racism. African Americans receive much harsher sentences than their white counterparts who do the same crime. Of course the majority of inmates on death row are African American. Racial profiling has swept the nation.

Even in sports, we remember the trials and tribulations of Jackie Robinson, Muhammad Ali and many others. Tiger Woods is of African American and Asian descent and the greatest golfer of all times. In spite of all of his achievements he still has to contend with racial hatred and discrimination.

In every area of our lives, race becomes the bottom line. This country is divided into red states and blue states. Ironically the red-blue divide falls along Confederate lines – it is slave states verses free states. A half a century later we have come full circle.

The progress that has been made in the past 50 years, especially the Voting Rights Act of 1965, is threatened by unfair rulings from the Supreme Court. They have ruled to gut a key provision of this act and have ruled to make it more difficult for employees to sue for racial discrimination.

So this is how the lay of the land looks in 2013. African Americans have gained some ground and have lost some ground. The losses are due to the dogged determination of white supremacists to not "let my people go."

I am not one given to joining boards but a few years ago I read that the city was looking for people to serve on a race relations task force. I called the mayor's office and joined. I received a two year commission to serve on this board. Because of my background in civil rights I thought I might have something to offer.

We were a mixed group and our chairman was an Hispanic American from Ecuador. He is classified as non-white, but he is also classified as non-black. Of course, the mayor appointed our chairman. We set about to see what other cities our size were doing to improve race relations. First, we had discussions about what should be done to make things better. An African American professor from the local university stood up and said that education is our problem. Basically, he said that if black people would get an education this would solve the problem. Of course I could not sit still for that. I said that many of us got the degrees but are still denied the opportunities. Another person said that economics is our problem and that black people need to pull themselves up by their bootstraps. I could not sit still for that either. I explained all about not having a level playing field and how many of us do not have any boots to begin with which is like saying you must "make bricks with no straw" as the Pharaoh told the Israelites to do in the book of Exodus. Some of the members were angry with my point of view. I felt as though I was, as the young folks say, "keeping it real."

At another meeting we discussed why so many black males do not have jobs. I asked our chairman, being from an Hispanic country, if he and an equally qualified black male applied for the same job opening who would most likely get the job? White males are hired over black males, white females are hired over black males even black females are hired over black males.

The group became adverse to using the words racist and racism. They began talking in terms of cultural diversification. I pointed out that white America is much more accepting of foreigners, like our chairman, than of African Americans. It is apples and oranges to try to say that culture and race are interchangeable. I perceived that they wanted to justify themselves by saying that if you like foreigners you are not a racist. I was "just keeping it real."

Needless to say I became a real thorn in their sides. We continued to study what other cities around the country were doing about race relations. Mostly all of the cities first began by putting out posters and bumper stickers saying the city does not tolerate discrimination based on race, color, creed, etc. This was the very first step to begin the process. We never did this. I asked many times when were we going to do the posters and get the message out? Some one told me that if the mayor ever put up a poster like that in city hall he would be run out of town. Nothing was ever done with this task force and eventually it fell by the wayside.

The 2010 Census shows that whites are no longer the majority in our town. Non-whites (African Americans, Asians and Hispanics) are now the majority. However, our city council and parish governing bodies totally exemplify life on the new plantation. The black members are so outnumbered that they basically have to take whatever the white power structure wants them to have.

For years now I have been opposing the most racist "festival" imaginable. This festival is held on city property and the festival organizers pay the city for beer and security but the city says they are not responsible for this festival. It is put on by a private club. They call it the Contraband Days Pirate Festival.

First of all I think we can all agree that "contraband" does not signify anything good. The definition of contraband is "illegal or prohibited trade; smuggling." We know that if the law catches someone with contraband they are going to jail. So why would someone call a festival "contraband?'

For the past 56 years, in the first two weeks in the month of May, this city has celebrated the Contraband Days Pirate Festival. It has been 56 years of insulting African Americans, women and Christians. A local group puts on this festival and dress up as pirates. They board a boat at the sea wall and fire cannons at the city. To open the festivities they come ashore at the sea wall and "force" the mayor to walk the plank (which real pirates never did). The mayor gives them the keys to the city and the pirates take over the city for two weeks. Their leader is the legendary pirate Jean Lafitte. The takeover of the city is followed by much revelry, carnival rides, food booths, live musical performances, a parade and other activities. The city hangs pirate banners all along the lakeshore to celebrate. This seems like a lot of fun and it would be if it were not so offensive for a number of reasons.

The first reason being slaves were known as "contraband." According to the Civil War Dictionary, "three slaves of a Virginia owner sought refuge at Fort Monroe, Va., on May '61 and the southerner demanded their return under the Fugitive Slave Acts. Ben Butler refused, saying that since Va. had seceded, she had no right to the Federal laws. In a report to the Sec. of War,

30 July '61, he referred to the salves as "contraband of war" and the name came into unofficial usage as the slang term for (African American) or slave. The idea of contraband as a doctrine disappeared after the passage of the Confiscation Acts." In Gallatin, Paine set up a large program of hiring free slaves to work in the hospitals, kitchens, and the fort. They lived in contraband camps. (Boatner, Mark Mayo. **The Civil War Dictionary.** New York, N.Y.: McKay c1988.). So they might as well call it the Slave Festival.

A group of us met with the local club to ask them to change the name. They flat out refused.

Secondly, we oppose this festival because pirates were and still are criminals. They looted, raped, killed and committed other crimes. They are making heroes of pirates. What an example for young people to follow, and we wonder why some children are so violent?

The third reason is that Jean Lafitte was a notorious slave trader. When I first wrote this in the local newspaper there were those who wanted to tar and feather me and run me out of town. The newspaper did its own research and published the fact that Jean Lafitte was a notorious slave trader. He sold many slaves to people living in this area who have streets named after them. His involvement in the battle of New Orleans is suspect and overshadowed by his well documented slave trading activities.

The fourth reason is that the skull and crossbones depicted in the pirates' logo is also known as the "Jolly Roger." There are a few theories about the origin of the term "Jolly Roger" but the most accepted is that the English commonly named their stud bulls "Roger". The word was already a term being widely used to describe sexual intercourse, usually of a vigorous nature. One of the characteristics of pirates was their brutal treatment of female prisoners that they had taken from other ships. They were commonly "rogered" to the rail by one and all and then thrown overboard.

The fifth reason is that the skull and crossbones is a satanic symbol. Not only has it flown on pirate ships as a sign of death, it was also chosen by the Nazis to be worn on their arm bands. You can also find it pictured on a bottle of poison.

Still there are those who do not care if contraband means slaves or illegal goods. There are those who see Jean Lafitte as a hero instead of a slave trader. There are those who refuse to accept the criminality of pirates. They say slavery was back then and they tell us to get over it. They say it is all in fun and has nothing to do with slavery. Wrong, it has everything to do with slavery. We, of African descent, honor the memory of our ancestors. We revere their memory, their courage, and their ability to survive against all odds. We are not about to condone dressing up like those who were responsible for inflicting bitter bondage on them. Just because the ancestors of white people did not come to these shores the same way that ours did does not give them the right to offend us. This disrespects their memory and makes light of what they had to suffer. This festival pours salt into open racial wounds that have not healed and will never heal as long as this goes on. It sends a strong message that white America does not feel our pain, does not even care if we have any pain. The message is that we should just keep our pain to ourselves while they have fun. It is the height of racial insensitivity.

If we are going to celebrate pirates we might as well go to the State Penitentiary and celebrate the thieves, rapists and murderers there. We could have a parade and a cook-off and call it "Criminal Appreciation Days." After all, a criminal is a criminal whether they wear a patch over one eye and a feather in his cap or prison stripes. Pirates have been glamorized in some books such as *Treasure Island* or *Peter Pan*. They have been romanticized by Hollywood in movies such as *Pirates of the Caribbean* staring Johnny Depp. Baseball and football teams are named after them. The fact of the matter is there is no such thing as a good pirate. It is an oxymoron. Dressing up like the bad guys, even in fun, has very negative connotations. It is impossible to turn the negative image of a pirate into something positive. To do this a disconnection and a desensitizing has to take place. This eventually results in obscuring the distinction between the good guys and the bad guys. That is confusing especially for young people who desperately need positive role models.

When I, as an African American woman stand at the Calcasieu River, I know that some of my ancestors were brought up that river by pirates – against their wills, torn from their motherland and their loved ones. They were not on a Carnival Cruise Ship and they were not coming to a land of freedom and opportunity. Far from it, they were brought here to literally work themselves to death making the slave owners rich.

When I look across that river I can hear them crying. They weep loudest once a year when people have the gall to imitate their captors and make a festival of it.

If the city was flying swastika flags down the lakeshore there would be an incredible outcry. Who would tell the Jews that the Holocaust is over, get over it? There is no celebration in this country making light of Hitler's regime or the German railways and customs. We demand respect for the memory of the sufferings of our ancestors and for ourselves.

We live in a racially divided city where the lingering effects of slavery have resulted in long-term racial inequalities and injustices. We have an abundance of housing, financial, educational, criminal justice and economic injustices. The Contraband Days Pirate Festival exacerbates this. On numerous occasions I have written articles in the local newspaper calling upon all people of good will, black and white, to work together to change the name of this festival and cease celebrating Jean Lafitte and pirates. We want a festival that uplifts the entire community – a festival that offends no one – a festival that is not divisive but is unifying.

Worse yet, there are a few African Americans who say they do not see anything wrong with the festival. I believe this is a monumental testament to their ignorance, indifference or just plain greed for a dollar. They should fall on their knees and ask forgiveness of our ancestors.

African Americans cannot make any progress in this city when someone is spitting in our faces two weeks out of every year – dishonoring the memory of African ancestors and treating our racial pride with total insensitivity. If we, as civil rights activists, roll over and even join with those who do this, we cannot expect any respect on the job, in education or anywhere else. If we do not fight for our racial dignity in something as basic as The Contraband Days Pirate Festival, any other fight is just a joke.

This year we decided to fight back with the greatest weapon we have: PRAYER. All of the armies in the world and all of the guns and tanks and bombs in the world cannot change people's hearts – but God can. We held a prayer vigil this year on the first day of the Contraband Days Pirate Festival. A group of us went down to the sea wall dressed as our African ancestors. I was dressed as Harriet Tubman, the new Moses of the Underground Railroad. Sojourner Truth was there, so was Frederick Douglas and others. We read the scriptures, rang the bells of freedom, lit the candles and threw roses in the water as a memorial. The roses were red for their blood and white as a token of God's love and of our love. This prayer vigil was called "Pray For Change."

We began our program in **REMEMBRANCE** saying: "We are gathered here today to honor the memory of every African, who at any time in history was torn from the motherland and forced into the bitter bondage of slavery in this country or in any country in the world. We commend their souls to God and ask God to have mercy on their souls and grant them eternal peace. In their earthly journey they uniquely shared in the sufferings of His only begotten son, Our Lord and Savior, Jesus Christ. May they one day reign with Him in the glorious resurrection. Amen. We also gather here today to pray for divine intervention to change the Contraband Days Pirate Festival. We ask God to open the eyes and move the hearts of those who put on this festival to change it to something we can all celebrate." We then had scripture readings and songs and the ringing of the bells of freedom while we called out the names of slave and freedom fighters in history. Following this we placed red and white roses in the water and said: "Accept these red roses dear souls as a token of our remembrance of your bitter bondage. Accept these white roses as a token of God's love and our love." Following this we lit candles and prayed: "Heavenly Father, as Jesus is our Light, shining in the darkness of this world, we know that you call each of us to be light. We believe that it is better to light one candle, in peace, than to curse the darkness. As you call each of us to be the light of Christ in our world, we pray that you fill us with the fire of the Holy Spirit and let our hearts burn with the fire of your perfect love in this cold dark world." We read more scripture and sang more songs. Finally, we prayed: "Merciful Father, as we gather here in memory of all African slaves, we want to have within us the heart of Our Lord and Savior, Jesus Christ, who after being brutally crucified, forgave his enemies from the cross. In imitation of Christ, we forgive all slave traders and slave owners. We commend their souls to you Almighty Father and God of us all. We know that healing begins with forgiveness and that there is no true healing for our land unless we first forgive. In the spirit of Jesus

Christ, make our hearts big enough and strong enough to forgive our oppressors, past and present. Breathe your spirit upon each and every one of us, Lord, upon this country, upon our parish, our state. Teach us to live in peace and harmony, with malice towards none and justice for all. With your divine charity, wipe out all hatred and racial discrimination from our community. We ask for your divine intervention in changing the Contraband Days Pirate Festival to a festival that is not offensive to anyone or to the memory of our African ancestors. Grant this through Our Lord and Savior Jesus Christ. Amen."

You do not have to be a rocket scientist to figure out that we do indeed live on the new plantation. Our African American community is suffering from a critical leadership crisis. We know we are living on the new plantation when we elect African Americans to political office and they soon learn that their political survival depends on how well they fall in line with the white power structure. In fact, African American "leadership" has been so manipulated by white political operatives, in most cases, I did not say in all, but in most cases, this manipulation has produced incompetent and ineffective "leaders.' This further reinforces the white view that African Americans are incapable of making intelligent decisions and determining our own progress and success. We know we are living on the new plantation when African Americans are afraid of retaliation if they take a stand that is not pleasing to the white power structure. We know we are living on the new plantation when African Americans are programmed to know their place. We know we are living on the new plantation when even African American churches are silent. We know we are living on the new plantation when the Contraband Days Pirate Festival is celebrated in our town. We know we are living on the new plantation when African Americans like to celebrate Black History Month and talk (talk only) about how Martin Luther King, Jr. had a dream. Martin Luther King, Jr. did not just talk about a dream of social, economic and educational justice. He sat in many jails for that dream. He put his life on the line for that dream. Working towards such a dream requires more than having a parade and a cook-off and hustling to make money off of anything that has MLK on it. I have a feeling that Dr. King rolls over in his grave every February when Black History Month comes around.

I wrote this little poem for black people who put money before their racial dignity:

Black Dreams

Black dreams hardly ever come true
because we dream in white.
We dream of having a white house
surrounded by a white picket fence,
a white Cadillac and a white fur coat.
Whitey jingles the change in his pocket
but we have no change and are seduced by the jingle.
Our soul is the price we pay for his jingle.
O foolish sons of Africa!

CHAPTER 5

We have the Power

*"If my people who are called by my name,
will humble themselves and pray and seek my
face and turn from their wicked ways, then I
will hear from heaven and will forgive their
sin and will heal their land. Now my eyes will
be opened and ears attentive to the prayers
offered in this place." 2 Chronicles 14-15*

Some of the most valuable lessons God ever taught me
came late in life. It was through trials and tribulations
that God revealed his power to me and taught me how
to rebuke the forces of evil in the Holy Name of Jesus.
The first and maybe the greatest trial came when my
husband and I had been very happily married for over
18 years. I began to see an addiction take over and
try to destroy the wonderful love of my life. We tried

every human resource available to us to free him of this addiction, including inpatient treatment. None of them worked. One day I looked him squarely in the face and I did not see the man I married. What I saw was some evil entity, apart from him but at the same time within him. God gave me to recognize that it was a demon. It did not frighten me but I was completely stunned by the fact that I could recognize it. My first thoughts went to God. I asked God what should I do? I told God that I have no idea of how to fight the devil trying to destroy a perfectly good man. How do I stop this? Right away God told me to look at the crucifix. "Look at the crucifix," he said to me, "because the victory is yours." He said that Jesus had already won the victory for me and my husband over this demon of addiction. Then he flashed a picture in my mind of a board being snapped in two and he said to me that this is how clean I will break this addition from him. We prayed and struggled with this for a while and until the day God took my husband's precious soul to heaven he never had another drink. He was 26 years free of alcohol addiction. God kept his word to me.

This was just the beginning in the spiritual lessons that God wanted to teach me regarding spiritual warfare. In 1986 my husband suffered a major stroke that he was not diagnosed to survive. Against all odds he survived and eventually walked and talked again. This catastrophic event eventually threw us into financial ruin. I was crying out to God about how I did not have the money to pay the auto insurance. Very clearly God said to me "I am the God over car insurance. I can fix it so that you will not need car insurance." Strange thing about this is that I did not understand what God meant by fixing it. I thought that God should send an angel to my door and give me the money. I learned that that is not how God works. The fact of the matter is I forgot all about these words and drove for months without car insurance until the day God gave us a new car. I never got a ticket, never got a fine. God fixed it.

One night I got a phone call from my very best friend. She was extremely distressed. There is a nightclub located at the corner from her house and the whole neighborhood was terrified. Fights and shootings were common at this nightclub. Through her window one night she saw two men lying in pools of blood in the parking lot of this nightclub. She went out there to pray for God to save their lives. When this nightclub was opened for business she and her son would have to hide under the furniture so that they would not be hit by bullets fired from this nightclub. One of her neighbors had 5 bullet holes in her back door. My friend told me that on certain nights her neighborhood was like the wild, wild west or a war zone. She asked me to help her do something about it.

We prayed and asked God to show us what to do to end this violence before someone would be killed. Amazingly what God showed us was that he was going to use us to bring peace to that neighborhood and that it was not our battle but the Lord's. My friend always says that God needs willing vessels to do his work in the world. We felt honored and humbled that God had chosen us to do his work.

We spoke with the local police department and found out that they had gotten a huge number of complaints against this club in the last few years. The police told us that our city councilman was aware of this but never took any action to correct it. When we spoke with the mayor he asked us if we knew that we have elected officials to take care of things like this? We answered that we elected them but they do not do what we elected them to do. We were told that the first action that we would need to take would be to have the club's alcohol license revoked by the Alcohol Board. This was not going to be easy. We were also told that the owner of the club was a drug dealer with connections. Everyone betrayed us – local politicians, friends, relatives, some law enforcement, even the terrified people in the neighborhood. They were too scared to open the door to talk with us let alone come to an Alcohol Board meeting. People asked us if we were afraid of the drug dealers and what they would do to us? Looking back I think we were too dumb to be scared. Then I think again that God had us on a mission and there was no room for fear in the picture. We went through months of delays and intimidation. Finally we testified before the Alcohol Board. They voted to take the club's liquor license. We celebrated and gave all praise and glory to God. The club decided to appeal this decision to the city council. The battle heated up. We made flyers and pleaded with the neighbors to come with us to testify before the city council about how much terror they were living in. They refused. One police officer who was with us from the beginning was the only person who did not desert us. Twice he came to my door to say that the drug dealers had sent someone to tell him to abandon us but he never did. We felt like David and Goliath. We had no political power or influence in the community to get people to rally to our cause.

The battle was not ours, the battle was the Lord's. By faith we knew that God is more powerful than politicians and drug dealers. So one day, my friend and I took our Bibles and went to that nightclub. We walked around that club seven times, as Joshua did fighting the battle of Jericho. We proclaimed the word of God, sang songs to God, and gave praise to God for winning the battle for us. Then after much rescheduling my friend and I testified before the city council. The city council voted to uphold the decision of the Alcohol Board. That club has been closed ever since. The people in the neighborhood (mostly elderly widows) thank us for bringing peace to their neighborhood. We tell them to give God the glory.

This is what I have learned from this and other events in my life – God is the answer, prayer is the answer. God has all of the power in heaven, on earth and under the earth. Once we tap into that power we can fully realize that nothing, absolutely nothing, is impossible with God – not even the eradication of racism.

When we went to the sea wall to pray for a change to the Contraband Days Pirate Festival the power and the presence of God was so thick in the air you could cut it with a knife. God confirmed to us that once we lifted up our hands to the heavens he sent the victory down. There is a saying that when praise goes up, blessings come down. This is the same message that God is giving regarding putting an end to racial hatred and discrimination. We must, individually and collectively lift our hands to heaven and cry out to God to change human hearts. No government or power on earth can change the human heart, only God can do that. "I will give you a new heart and place a new spirit within you, taking from your bodies your stony hearts and giving you natural hearts." Ezekiel 36:26. Government is not our savior. God is our savior.

God is love and racial hatred is non-love right straight out of the pits of evil. We rebuke it in the Holy Name of Jesus. We rebuke it from our lives, from our cities, from our states, from our country, from the world. "Beloved, let us love one another, because love is of God; everyone who loves is begotten by God and knows God, for God is love." 1 John 4:7-8.

Love has to be the most misunderstood word in the English language. It is often confused with infatuation or lust and is characterized by displays of affection. Most people describe love as an intense emotional feeling.

Biblical love is not about what we feel but about what we do. The love that God is calling us to have is not about how we feel but about what we do.

What is God telling us in the Bible about the kind of love we are to have? What does the word mean? To understand this we need to know a little bit about translating from one language to another. The New Testament was written in Greek. In Greek there are three words for love. In English there is only one word for all three definitions. The first Greek word is agape. The second is phileo. The third is eros.

Agape love is a common form of biblical love. It is sacrificial love – regardless of what is reciprocated. It drives one to save the helpless, even one's enemies. Agape love means doing or caring for someone as much as you do or care for yourself. Agape love needs no incentive and does not ask "what do I get out of it?" It focuses on how you can meet the needs of others. Agape love is self-sacrificial: "Greater love has no one than this, than he lay down his life for his friends." John 15:13. This is Godly love and can be manifested even if you do not like or know someone. Only God can completely give this kind of love: "For God so loved the world that he gave his only begotten son." John 3:16.

Phileo love is brotherly love. Humans, without the indwelling of the Holy Spirit, can give this love for God or their fellow man. Phileo love is a befriending love. You have a fondness for them. You treat them with signs of love.

The third is eros. It pertains to sex and is not in the Bible but translates from classical Greek writings.

God's love (agape love) is unconditional and our love, which is phileo love is not. One trivia point is that Philadelphia is known as the city of brotherly love and this is taken from the Greek, phileo.

One of the greatest biblical accounts of the difference between agape love and phileo love is found in John 21:15 where Jesus asks Peter three times if he loves him. At the third time Peter becomes a little exasperated that Jesus kept repeating the question but most of all he was ashamed of himself for denying him. On the night when Jesus was handed over, three times

Peter denied that he even knew him. He had shortly before told Jesus that he would give his life for him, but when the chips were down, he denied him, three times. Peter was ashamed that he could not bring himself to acknowledge agape love for Jesus. He could only admit preferring Jesus as a friend. He failed to demonstrate agape love. In the end, however, we know that he did have agape love for Jesus and died a martyr. He was crucified upside down because he said that he was not worthy to die right side up on the cross as Jesus did.

We learn of the origin of love in 1 John, Chapter 4, verses 7-9: "Beloved let us love one another, because love is of God; everyone who loves is begotten by God and knows God. Whoever is without love does not know God, for God is love." He has given us the capacity for love. The capacity for love is one of the ways that we are created in the image of God.

"I give you a new commandment: Love one another. As I have loved you, so you also should love one another. This is how all will know that you are my disciples, if you have love for one another." John 13:34-36.

Mahatma Gandhi is one of the most respected leaders in modern history. He was a devout Hindu but he greatly admired Jesus Christ. He often quoted from the Sermon on the Mount and they say that in his office, over his desk, hung a huge, beautiful picture of Jesus, not of Budha or Krishna, but of Jesus. He admired Jesus so much, people often asked him why he was not a Christian? He would reply "Oh, I don't reject your Christ. I love your Christ. It's just that so many of you Christians are so unlike your Christ."

Jesus did not have to stamp our foreheads or put some other markings on us to show that we are his followers. He said that they will know that you belong to me and follow me by the way you have love one for another. I can understand what Gandhi meant. I cannot tell the difference between Christian, pagan, Jews, Muslim, Hindu or any other religion. This means that Christians are not looking like Jesus wants us to look to the world. Most Christians think that it is good enough to love your family, love your friends, don't kill anybody and that should be enough. But Jesus, the Great Disturber, says in Matthew 5:46-48: "For if you love those who love you, what recompense will you have? Do not the tax collectors do the same? And if you greet your brother only, what is unusual about that? Do not the pagans do the same?" He showed the epitome of agape love for us. He hung on that cross, naked, bleeding, covered with spit and blood and even asked his father to forgive his murderers. He gave all he had to give for us.

We are called to agape love. We are called to love greatly. We probably will not be crucified but we are called to love as Jesus loved. We are called to come out of our comfort zones and let the world know by our love that we are his faithful followers: "We know that we have passed from death to life because we love our brothers. Whoever does not love remains in death. Everyone who hates his brother is a murderer, and you know that no murderer has eternal life remaining in him. The way that we came to know love was that he laid down his life for us, so we ought to lay down our lives for our brothers." 1 John 3:11-17.

This reminds me of Scrooge and Marley in Charles Dickens *A Christmas Carol*. The ghost of Jacob Marley appears to Scrooge laden down with chains and irons. Scrooge asks Marley why is he wearing chains and irons? Marley replies that he is wearing the irons as a result of what he forged in life. Scrooge protests and says "but you were always a good man of business, Jacob," to which Marley replies "business

– mankind was my business – the common welfare was my business, charity, mercy, forbearance, and benevolence were all my business."

In order to live Biblical love, agape love, humankind must be our business. Social justice is rooted in agape love. We act justly toward one another out of love. Our love must translate into working for justice. "Our God is a God of justice and calls us to act justly and to love mercy and to walk humbly before Him." Micah 6:8.

There are statues of justice called "Lady Justice or "Blind Justice." She is holding a sword in one hand and a scale in the other and is blindfolded. The symbols are to depict impartiality, devotion to objective truth and the need to weight different sides of the case. The reason why we are on the battlefield of justice is because American justice is neither blind nor fair. The scales are weighted against African Americans.

So many attitudes and preconceived ideas about one another cause us not to have love for one another. If a person of one race thinks that they are ok but someone of a different race is not there is the absence of even phileo love: "How can you say you love God whom you can't see if you can't love your neighbor who you can see?" 1 John 4:20-21.

Sadly, we must admit that there is racism among Christians, among Catholics and in the church. Like Gandhi it is scandalous to see this un-Christ-like attitude and behaviors. Of course things have improved considerably through the years, but not enough. I am a Lector in my church and I remember serving Mass, on the altar with white Eucharistic Ministers who I would later see in the supermarket with their friends. They acted as though they had never seen be before in their lives. I remember white people walking out of Mass when a black priest came to the altar to say the Mass. Now I am not passing judgment but I think they have a big surprise in store on judgment day. When God says depart from me, I never knew you and they will say: "Hold on God – didn't I give to the St. Vincent DePaul fund? Didn't I serve dinners to the hungry at Thanksgiving and Christmas? Didn't I tithe one tenth? Didn't I serve as a Eucharistic Minister on the altar? Didn't I buy Girl Scout cookies? Didn't I give to the United Way? And God will answer: "Depart from me, I never knew you. You never came out of your comfort zone. You did charity because it made you feel good. Your good feeling is your reward." It never ceases to amaze me how love is confused with charity. In 1

Corinthians St. Paul was not confused when he writes: "If I give all that I possess to the poor, but do not have love, I am nothing."

I recall a distinguished looking gentleman in one of my ministry classes. He looked like the successful business type. Every week the lesson would say how God wants us to help the poor. Well along about the third lesson this gentleman had taken about as much of that as he was going to take and he asked: "Who are these people? Are we supposed to go out looking for these poor people and give them money? Aren't there government programs to help these people?" Again, Scrooge in Charles Dickens *A Christmas Carol* comes to mind. The town elders came to Scrooge to ask for a donation for poor families at Christmas time. Scrooge asks: "Aren't there any poor houses or prisons to take care of these people?" He also said that he gave to the benevolent fund which would be our modern day United Way.

While we have an obligation to do Christian charity, we have an even greater obligation to share from our spiritual storehouse. Most of the time, agape love does not cost a dime. Sacrificing ourselves is the price that God wants us to pay. We need to take a stand and help the people of our community. We have to care about someone we don't even know and probably would not like even if we did know them. We must give of our time and ourselves. This is what God is asking of us. Turn off the television and help somebody. Help your wife, help your husband, help the old lady down the street, help your other family members, help your friends. This is a cold, cruel world. They need you more than you know. They need a word of encouragement. They need hope. If all you have to give is a smile, give it. Come out of your shell, your comfort zone and ask – what can I do for you today? If you are truly carrying God in your heart they need to know it not with words, but by your sacrificial love, by your agape love. Biblical love is not about what we say but about what we do.

St. Paul is very clear about the value of love: "If I speak in human and angelic tongues but do not have love, I am a resounding gong or a clashing cymbal. And if I have the gift of prophecy and comprehend all mysteries and all knowledge; if I have all faith so as to move mountains, but do not have love, I am nothing. If I give away everything I own, and if I hand my body over so that I may boast but do not have love, I gain nothing." 1 Corinthians, Chapter 13.

Some years ago, my husband and I both decided to become charismatic Catholics. This came from the desire that we both had to have a closer walk with God. We participated in the seminar to learn what the movement was about. On the eve of Pentecost we were baptized in the Holy Spirit. It opened up a whole new spiritual world for us – a world of living fully in the power of God that is given to every baptized Christian.

At baptism every Christian receives the gifts of the Holy Spirit. Catholic doctrine defines these gifts of the Holy Spirit as charisms. At our Confirmation we were to activate these charisms in our Christian life. We went a step further and we were baptized in the Holy Spirit. We have two baptisms. We were first baptized into Christ by water. Then we received Spirit baptism which is the charismatic power to be an effective witness (evangelizer) in building up the kingdom of God. Jesus said that we should be born again of water and the spirit: "Jesus answered, 'Amen, amen, I say to you, no one can enter the kingdom of God without being born of water and Spirit.'" John 3:5.

When Jesus ascended to his Father he gave his apostles tools to carry on his mission. Before they received the Holy Spirit they were powerless, uneducated and frightened. After they received the power of the Holy Spirit they had the power, the fire and the courage to go out and win the world for Jesus Christ. We owe our faith to them. We, who are baptized into the church, receive the same gifts and power as the apostles. I recently heard televangelist Joyce Myers say that baptized Christians receive the same powers as the apostles. The difference, she says is that they used them. "The man who has faith in me will do the works that I do, and greater far than these." John 14:22. We have the power!

Power is the ability or capacity to perform or act effectively. It is also defined as strength or force exerted or capable of being exerted. God is almighty, unmitigated power. Through baptism, Confirmation and baptism in the Holy Spirit, we share in God's power. He enables us to do things far greater than our human abilities. We know that there is no power greater than the power of God. No matter what the circumstance, we have the power. To heal our bodies and to lay hands on the sick and heal them – we have the power. To heal broken relationships – we have the power. To escape financial crisis – we have the power. To raise the dead – we have the power. To end racial hatred and discrimination – we have the power. No matter how impossible it seems, God can change it in an instant. To doubt this is to limit the almighty power of God, which has no limits. "These signs will accompany those who believe in my name: In my name they will drive out demons, they will speak new languages. They will pick up serpents (with their hands), and if they drink any deadly thing, it will not harm them. They will lay hands on the sick, and they will recover." Mark 16: 17-18.

This power is given to us to enable us to accomplish God's work. God empowers ordinary people like you and me. These charisms are not a sign of personal holiness but of the Holy Spirit working in and through ordinary people. God's promises are not just for those who are saintly or for those who have great authority or knowledge of the Bible. God's promises are for those who believe, for any Christian, for you and everyone of you. This is how God works – through ordinary people. God did not love the Apostles more than he loves you or I. He did not brand them a special people and give them something that he would not give us and God is extremely generous – these gifts are free. We cannot earn them. We don't deserve them. They are freely given to us by God.

God wants us to live in the power zone, in the empowerment of the Holy Spirit, in resurrection power – being Spirit-filled and fired up. When we live in this outpouring of the Holy Spirit we can do the work that God wants us to do for the good of the whole Body of Christ. Then we will see people's lives radically changed. Then we will see people healed. Then we will see demons sent away cowering like whipped puppies. Then we will see cities and nations awakened to a sense of repentance. Then we will finally see an end to racial hatred and discrimination. Then we will see even the dead come to life. We are champions of faith in the Holy Name of Jesus Christ and in that name we have the power.

I know so many people who just seem to accept being powerless. It brings to mind the story of the eagle. On a farm a large tree grew so that its branches overlapped over the chicken yard. A family of eagles came and made their nest in a large branch that grew over the chicken yard. One day, a baby eagle fell out of the nest and onto the chicken yard. He grew up in the confinements of the chicken yard and pecking at the ground all day long. He thought he was a chicken. From time to time he would look up and see the eagles soaring to the heavens. One day another eagle flew by and spotted him in the chicken yard. He said, hey, you are not a chicken, you are an eagle. Try to fly, you'll see. The eagle flapped his wings a little and started to fly, then he flapped them even more and took off. Before you know it he was soaring to the heavens like the rest of the eagles and he was free of that chicken yard. The moral of the story is that too many of us act like chickens when God made us to be eagles soaring to the heavens. We become so accustomed to the confines, restrictions, limitations of the chicken yard that we do not know how to get out, or worse yet, if we want to get out.

We are the light of the world. "You are the light of the world. A city set on a mountain cannot be hidden. Nor do they light a lamp and then put it under a bushel basket; it is set on a lampstand, where it gives light to all in the house. Just so, your light must shine before others, that they may see your good deeds and glorify your heavenly Father." Matthew 5: 14-16. I do not like one of the songs that we sing all of the time. The song is "This Little Light of Mine, I'm going to Let It Shine." I think that song should be stricken from every hymnal. Too many of us are satisfied with being just a little light. The operative word here is "little." In some instances the light is so little it is down to a flicker. The slightest breeze can snuff it out. This song, unintentionally, of course, promotes mediocrity and the tepid life. God has some harsh words for those who live the tepid life, the mediocre life. "I know your works; I know that you are neither cold nor hot. I wish that you were either cold or hot. So because you are lukewarm, neither hot nor cold, I will spit you out of my mouth." Revelations 3:15-16.

God has given us the power and the weapons to do good and overcome evil in the world. As Christians we must be aware that there are unseen, non-physical, supernatural forces in revolt against God and God's people. Jesus has defeated these forces but they still try to make us turn away from God. Everyday we must be ready to engage in spiritual warfare. We sing "Onward Christian Soldiers." It fires us up emotionally to fight the good fight – whatever that might be. In reality, we do not like war. We really, really do not like war

– especially the thought of ongoing, continuous warfare. In fact, unless we are some sicko warmongers we are not supposed to like war. Personally, I have a peaceful nature and the thought of fighting is distasteful to me.

At the Last Supper Jesus said "Peace I leave with you, my peace I give to you." John 14:27-28. The question is if we are engaged in perpetual, spiritual warfare, what happened to our peace?

Peace in the political realm means the absence of war. This kind of peace means the cessation of hostilities – not the end of hostility. As we learned from past generations – even when the hot war shuts down, a cold war may rage on, like Korea and Vietnam.

Christian peace is different from world peace. Jesus gives us his peace as a gift. It is not something we can get for ourselves by work.

Jesus gives us the "peace that surpasses understanding" Phillippians 4:7. The peace that Jesus gives brings calm in the face of trouble and it overcomes fear. The odd thing about the life of the Christian is that we are at war and at peace at the same time, also it is believed that the more we are engaged in spiritual warfare, the more our peace increases. Generally, when we think of spiritual warfare we think of exorcisms and heads turning around 360 degrees. This is an intense level of spiritual warfare that requires guidance from the Church. As a matter of fact I recently read that the Catholic Church has ordered and commissioned the training of more priests to perform exorcisms because demonic possessions have increased. Priests must be specially trained for this.

There is a tug of war going on for our souls. The reality of Christian life is that we know that our side wins. Jesus has won the victory for us but God wants us to fight this battle. Throughout scripture it is clear that God wants us to engage in spiritual warfare against the enemies of our eternal salvation. Why does God want us to do this? The first reason is because he wants us to win souls for him and the second is because he wants to make us saints.

When we were baptized, we enlisted in the Army of the Lord. Every Easter, we re-enlist. In the liturgy when it is time for the Creed the priest asks: "Do you renounce Satan and all his works and all his lies and tricks?" And we reply "I do." When we say "I do." We are throwing down the gauntlet. The line is being drawn in the sand. We are enlisted in the Army of God

– Jesus Christ is our Commander and Chief – Jesus Christ is our General and the Captain of our souls. The Bible is our marching orders. The whole battle plan is in the Book and our victory is in the Book.

One spiritual instructor put it this way: "When we are conceived the battle begins for our immortal soul." He says that we are born into a war zone and when we were baptized we were fitted with combat boots. When we became a child of God, we became an enemy of Satan. Welcome to the Church Militant. Jesus needs a few good men and women and teenagers and children.

Now that we are enlisted, how do we go to battle? "Finally, draw your strength from the Lord and from his mighty power. Put on the armor of God so that you may be able to stand firm against the tactics of the devil. For our struggle is not with flesh and blood but with the principalities, with the powers, with the world rulers of this present darkness, with the evil spirits in the heavens. Therefore, put on the armor of God, that you may be able to resist on the evil day and, having done everything, to hold your ground. So stand fast with your loins girded in truth, clothed with righteousness as a breastplate, and your feet shod in readiness for the gospel of peace. In all circumstances, hold faith as a shield, to quench all [the] flaming arrows of the evil one. And take the helmet of salvation and the sword of the Spirit, which is the word of God." Ephesians 6:10-18.

God has his soldiers well armed and well prepared. We have been given authority to come against the power of the enemy. It is important when we pray to place ourselves specifically under the Lord's protection and take authority over any power of evil in the Holy Name of Jesus.

We must be the hands and feet of Jesus in the world. All people of God, but especially those called to lead the people of God, must bring Christ to a hungry, thirsty, hurting world. There is a song that says that Christ has no other hands but ours. He is depending on us and especially upon religious leaders. "Woe to the shepherds who mislead and scatter the flock of my pasture, says the Lord." Jeremiah 23:1. I have my own list of woes. Woe to the shepherds who do not know the Christ they are called to preach. Woe to the shepherds who have become worldly and materialistic. Woe to the shepherds who are compromised with politics and have traded the truth for a lie. Woe to the shepherds who despise the poor and treat them with disdain. Woe to the shepherds who do not comprehend or preach the sacrificial love of Jesus Christ. Woe to the shepherds who do not unceasingly preach against the sin of racial hatred and discrimination. Woe to the shepherds who profess to have faith in God but do not do the works of God. Woe to the shepherds who lead the faithful astray out of ignorance or greed. Woe to the shepherds who despise the humiliation of the cross of Jesus Christ. Woe to the shepherds who out of fear or laziness water down the Word of God.

We know so well how racial hatred has permeated our nation. So when is the last time your pastor preached against racial hatred and discrimination? When is the last time your pastor said let us all join hands and pray for an end to racial hatred in our community, in our nation and in our world? Racism has become the elephant in the pews.

In years past, the black church was at the forefront of the civil rights movement. In my town, many non-Catholic churches have become agents against change and progress for African Americans. They establish these little neighborhood dynasties that are principally for the enrichment of the pastor. The pastors are motivated by money to hang on to their little kingdoms. Some of them have grown into big, expensive kingdoms. The parishioners live in spiritual isolation and are taught, in some instances, to look down on African Americans who are Catholic because they have been told that it is the white man's religion. They, like so many televangelists, preach the gospel of prosperity. They conveniently skip over the part where Jesus says that you cannot serve God and money. For them, storing up treasurers on earth is the primary goal of faithful living. Their followers strive for the trappings of luxury to prove they are blessed spiritually. The idea is that if you pray right God will make you rich. I have a huge book of the lives of saints who were faithful to God all of their lives, but very, very few of them were rich. As a matter of fact they found material things distracted them from their consecration to God. I disagree with the idea if you are not rich that you are not faithful to God. Jesus was born poor and he died poor. He came to save our souls not our financial portfolios.

As a civil rights advocate, I sometimes get a little upset with preachers and priests and religious leaders when a political election comes around. The least they could do is to make sure that their people get out and vote. Black voter apathy is disgraceful. We try to get into the churches to beg and plead for everyone to register and vote. Time after time, once the election is over and we review the results by precincts, the black precincts have the lowest turnout of all. We do not want to tell people how to vote we just want them to exercise their hard earned right to vote. I have seen how the non-vote can shift American politics. In November 1994 the horrendous Contract with America was the will of only one-third of the American people, yet it became the law of the land because the other two-thirds did not care enough to vote.

The voting booth is the great equalizer. In the voting booth there is no rich man, poor man, white man, black man. Everyone's vote carries the same weight. All votes are equal. If you do not vote you give someone else power over your life. There is only one thing that can stop billionaires from buying an election and that is your vote.

We must never forget Rev. George W. Lee who was slain May 7, 1956 in Belzoni, Mississippi. He was the first black to register to vote in his county. He was killed for refusing to remove his name from the voter polls. James Chaney was slain June 1964 in Philadelphia, Mississippi, along with white co-workers Michael Schwerner and Andrew Goodman, registering voters. All three were beaten and shot to death. Jimmy Lee Jackson was slain February 1965 in Marion, Alabama. He was injured while attempting to protect his mother from being beaten by an Alabama State Trooper following police invasion of a voter registration rally. He died 12 days later. Medgar W. Evers was slain June 12, 1963 in Jackson, Mississippi. He was a leader in voter registration. He was shot from ambush in front of his home. Dr. Martin Luther King, Jr., leader of the Selma, Alabama march that brought about the Voting Rights Act of 1965 was shot to death by a sniper. The blood cries out against voter apathy and voter suppression. That their blood should not have been shed in vain, every person who is able to, should vote. We have a saying in the civil rights struggle: "A vote-less people is a hope-less people."

The religious "leaders" have become so accustomed to the sinful state of racial hatred that they are immune to it. Some want it to go away, but they do not intend to do anything to make that happen. Racism is a scourge on American society but they do not want to do anything to rock the boat or make waves. Let someone else do it. If they started preaching like this they might get less money in the collection plate. The bishop might call them out and remove them from their church. The fear is paralyzing.

There should be a fervent prayer every Sunday in every church for an end to racial hatred and discrimination. When the power of these prayers goes up to God, he will be moved to change human hearts. Do we have faith in the power of prayer, especially united prayer? Jesus was not just blowing smoke when he called us to be the light of the world and the salt of the earth. We have the power. We are not chickens, we are eagles.

Knowing that God is love, the faithful Christian knows that hate comes from the devil. Jesus, on the cross, has defeated Satan. In His Holy Name we claim victory over racial hatred and discrimination. We have the power and the victory in keeping our hands lifted to God in prayer: "So Joshua did as Moses told him: he engaged Amalek in battle after Moses had climbed to the top of the hill with Aaron and Hur. As long as Moses kept his hands raised up, Israel had the better of the fight, but when he let his hands rest, Amalek had the better of the fight. Moses' hands, however, grew tired; so they put a rock in place for him to sit on. Meanwhile, Aaron and Hur supported his hands, one on one side and one on the other, so that his hands remained steady until sunset. And Joshua mowed down Amalek and his people with the edge of the sword." Exodus 17:10-13.

Where there is no peace, there is no Jesus. Jesus came as the Prince of Peace. He came to teach us how to love and to give us peace. "Peace I leave with you; my peace I give to you. Not as the world gives do I give it to you. Do not let your hearts be troubled or afraid." John 14:27. Today, we claim that peace for ourselves, our families, our cities, our states, our nation, our world as we pray the prayer of Saint Francis of Assisi:

Lord, make me an instrument of Your peace: Where there is hatred let me sow love, where there is injury, pardon, where there is doubt, faith, where there is despair, hope, where there is darkness, light, where there is sadness, joy. O Divine Master, grant that I may not so much seek to be comforted as to comfort, to be understood as to understand,

to be loved as to love. Because it is in giving that
we receive, it is in pardoning that we are pardoned,
and it is in dying that we are born to eternal life.

May the peace of the Lord be always with us.
Amen.

Bibliography

Asante, Molefi, Kete. *Erasing Racism: The Survival of the American Nation*. Amherst, New York: Prometheus Books, 2003.

Bonilla-Silva. *White Supremacy and Racism in the Post-Civil Rights Era*. Boulder, Colorado: Lynne Riemer Publishers, Inc., 2001.

Johnson, Elizabeth A. *Consider Jesus*. New York: Crossroad, 1997.

Stone, Bryan P. *Compassionate Ministry*. Maryknoll, New York: Orbis Books, 1996.

Wallis, Jim. *The Soul of Politics*. Maryknoll New York: Orbis Books, 1994